Empowering Children through Art and Expression

of related interest

Expressive and Creative Arts Methods for Trauma Survivors
Edited by Lois Carey
ISBN 978 1 84310 386 8

Shattered Lives
Children Who Live with Courage and Dignity
Camila Batmanghelidjh
ISBN 978 1 84310 434 6

The Child's Own Story
Life Story Work with Traumatized Children
Richard Rose and Terry Philpot
Foreword by Mary Walsh, co-founder and Chief Executive of SACCS
ISBN 978 1 84310 287 8

Reaching the Vulnerable Child
Therapy with Traumatized Children
Janie Rymaszewska and Terry Philpot
Foreword by Mary Walsh, co-founder and Chief Executive of SACCS
ISBN 978 1 84310 329 5

The Handbook of Gestalt Play Therapy
Practical Guidelines for Child Therapists
Rinda Blom
Foreword by Hannie Schoeman
ISBN 978 1 84310 459 9

Arts Therapists, Refugees and Migrants
Reaching Across Borders
Edited by Ditty Dokter
ISBN 978 1 85302 550 1

Children's Stories in Play Therapy
Ann Cattanach
ISBN 978 1 85302 362 0

Clayworks in Art Therapy
Plying the Sacred Circle
David Henley
ISBN 978 1 84310 706 4

Empowering Children through Art and Expression

Culturally Sensitive Ways of Healing Trauma and Grief

Bruce St Thomas and Paul Johnson

Jessica Kingsley Publishers
London and Philadelphia

Jessica Kingsley Publishers
116 Pentonville Road
London N1 9JB, UK
and
400 Market Street, Suite 400
Philadelphia, PA 19106, USA

www.jkp.com

Library of Congress Cataloging in Publication Data
St. Thomas, Bruce, 1948-
   Empowering children through art and expression : culturally sensitive ways of healing trauma and grief / Bruce St. Thomas and Paul Johnson.
      p. ; cm.
   Includes bibliographical references and indexes.
   ISBN 978-1-84310-789-7 (alk. paper)
   1. Art therapy for children. 2. Creation (Literary, artistic, etc.)—Therapeutic use. 3. Grief in children—Treatment. 4. Psychic trauma in children—Treatment. 5. Post-traumatic stress disorder in children—Treatment. I. Johnson, Paul (Paul Gordon), 1959- II. Title.
   [DNLM: 1. Sensory Art Therapies—methods. 2. Child Psychology—methods. 3. Child. 4. Culture. 5. Stress Disorders, Post-Traumatic—therapy. WM 450 S774e 2007]
   RJ505.A7S72 2007
   618.92'89165—dc22

                                                        2007007808

British Library Cataloguing in Publication Data
A CIP catalogue record for this book is available from the British Library

ISBN 978 1 84310 789 7

Printed and bound in the United States of America by Thomson-Shore, Inc.

Contents

List of Figures

Acknowledgments

A special thanks goes out to all of the unique community peer support programs that we have had the privilege to draw from in this writing. The Center for Grieving Children and its Multicultural Program in Portland, Maine has been foundational to our work and findings. A special thanks to Anne Lynch, Director, Linda Kelly, Program Director and Marie Sheffield, Art Therapy/Mental Health Consultant, who has helped in providing specific stories, images and collaborations. The philosophy and practices of the Multicultural Program have been supportive to our theories, writing and findings.

A special thanks goes out to America's Camp. The camp's directors, Andy Cole, Jay Toporoff, Danny Metzgar and Jed Dorfman, well appreciate the developmental and camping needs that are necessary in providing children who have experienced a very complex grief with the opportunity for fun and community support. Also a thank you is extended to Laurence Levy who organizes and administers the America's Camp Foundation making this camp possible, and to Traci Molloy, resident artist, who developed the community-based art activities that serve as an important form of peer communication as well as a history regarding the transformation of grief. To the many counselors, buddies, program staff and support staff we also extend our gratitude for their loving commitment and undaunting positive regard for this community.

A special thanks to Work Opportunities Unlimited and especially to Susan Abel, Executive Director, and to Anne Dobson, Rehabilitation Counselor and Group Facilitator. We also wish to thank Arthur Fink, for all his technical assistance with the images for this book. A deep gratitude and love goes out to both of our wives; without the "Pegs" supporting us we would be unable to accomplish our goal. They have sacrificed many hours for the much needed times in compiling this writing.

Preface

In January 2000, Bruce and I met for the first time at the Center for Grieving Children, in Portland, Maine. Little did we realize at that first meeting, that over the course of the next six years we would embark on the journey of writing this book. What was very apparent from our first meeting was that we had many parallel and common experiences. The first was that our wives had the same name, Peg. If this wasn't a good omen then I didn't know what was. However, what transpired was just amazing. Both of us in our professional careers had worked with children, families and communities, where trauma and grief had been key components. Each of us talked about how we had gained a deeper appreciation for loss and tragedy. Bruce had been trained in psychotherapy as well as art therapy. I had been trained as a social worker in England. Each of us had worked in a variety of different settings. For example Bruce had been a mental health professional in the US Army, I had worked with the physically and mentally challenged both in the United Kingdom and in the United States.

Both of these experiences had a profound impact upon us. For example in Bruce's case this was a time when Post Traumatic Stress Disorder (PTSD) wasn't even conceptualized; there was collaborative support within the psychiatric and medical community to support complex issues of quadriplegic amputees, burn patients and psychological war-time trauma. In my case, the work that I was undertaking with physically and mentally handicapped individuals and their families had a profound impact upon me. The profound sense of loss that the families experienced, the difficulties of just getting through the day and dealing with basic issues of dressing, toileting, feeding, were monumental. With both these groups there was a great sense of suffering and impairment. We had both worked in settings where change seemed unimaginable. Yet in both situations we had observed the human ability to transform.

Following these experiences both of us moved into work that was more child and family focused, Bruce as a psychotherapist and art therapist, I as a social worker in a child welfare agency. Again, what amazed me in working with these children and families was the stories they would tell. In social work we talk about "empowering of the client," "being where the client is." However, I was always amazed at not only what these children and families would tell me, but also how through modalities such as board games, and art materials that I kept in my office, they would tell me such complex and detailed stories. They would use these modalities as a vehicle to tell their innermost thoughts. I also found that when I went out for a walk with the children or visited them in their home, I gained a greater insight into their lives. They would share with me stories they had written for a school project, tell me about their friends, favorite team, or group. Tell me about their mothers, fathers, brothers, sisters, aunts, uncles and grandparents. The stories just kept flowing.

Bruce also informed me that through his own work he too had been amazed at the stories children had told. However, what would change his understanding of the natural process of self-healing forever would be the thousands of stories and re-enactments naturally expressed by children and families through art, drama, hands-on materials and puppets. From their bodies and minds came the age-old myths, legends and folklores. Instinctive was the child's ability not only to play out the pain and struggle of specific trauma and loss but also to find resolution through the highly complex matrix of knowing and inventing new connections to create meaning, insight and resolution. The leap that children took into the mythic world was automatic once the trust and safety had been well established. Working with highly traumatized children, Bruce experienced very often their narrative ability to re-enter the fearful and difficult place in their own trauma story with the use of metaphor, art and drama which would often include familiar fairy tale themes. Playing with the archetypal characters such as the King, Queen, Princess, Prince, Sprite, Wizard, Witch and any array of symbols from nature as well as the animal kingdom, children would re-enact themes from their own life and trauma. Abandonment, survivor guilt, loss of control, recovering from the shock or pain, expressing anger, guilt, sadness, disbelief, love, would all emerge from the art and dramatic play. Children knew how to put their healing into action.

It is hard to say how or why we connected, but for me talking to Bruce was like a breath of fresh air. I finally had met someone who viewed the world the same way as I did. When I would talk about the insight of the child and the ability to self-heal, it was if I finally had someone who agreed with me. Each week we would meet at a coffee house in Portland, we would talk for hours. Bruce talked about the Center for Grieving Children and the Multicultural Program. How the program utilized art and play. He also talked about the children leading the healing process and how many professionals and non-professionals felt unfamiliar with these concepts.

Over the course of the next five years we wrote several articles together, presented at local, national and international conferences. We also talked about our own childhoods, my growing up in England and Bruce's formative years in rural Maine. We talked about what a profound impact our families had had upon each of us. We further explored how each of us had gained enough self-assurance and hope to tackle life's challenges. We dialogued about our abilities to remain in touch with childhood strengths even into our adult lives. Indeed Chapter Ten of the book provides a detailed account of our own childhoods.

What was very apparent to both of us was just how resourceful and insightful the child is. Unfortunately, today it appears that children are often not recognized or valued as being insightful. Rather, they are viewed as being a blank slate in need of training and learning. Our experiences have contradicted this viewpoint. We view the child as being extremely creative, possessing a great deal of insight and knowing what he or she needs to do in order to bring about self-healing.

This book is the culmination of years of experience whereby such genius, wisdom, flexibility and insight has shaped our understanding of how internal change occurs. Experiencing such truthful stories and enactments has shaped our practice. This book's intention is to engage both the clinical and non-clinical reader in a deeper appreciation of the instinctive power inherent in the child's natural ability to heal unintegrated traumatic events.

Capturing the complex path to trust and healing is no easy task. Yet, the stories and events shared in this writing help the reader to understand that being present, accepting the unusual, letting go of outcomes, promoting creative expression and being available to build trust and safety are essential building blocks in facilitating healing. Throughout this writing readers will gain both an appreciation and understanding of the importance of creativity, spontaneity and affective expression.

This book will help to underscore why body-centered, free expression is critical in building awareness as well as integrating trauma. Children have an uncanny ability to draw directly from the unconscious content of their life stories and events. Instinctively children hold pleasure over principle which affords them the opportunity to play with the unimaginable. Most trauma victims find it impossible to describe or put into words their most personal pain and anguish. This book demonstrates that by using child-centered activities the ineffable can both be expressed and integrated.

Paul Johnson

Introduction

Globally, human conflict and struggle around the issues of terrorism, genocide, civil wars, disregard for human life, political upheaval, economic instability, human disease, the demise of eco-systems, and natural disasters are creating an unprecedented awareness of our human interdependence and vulnerability. Seldom do written documents look toward children for the insights and answers. *Empowering Children through Art and Expression: Culturally Sensitive Ways of Healing Trauma and Grief* explores the inter-relationship between childhood trauma, the power of play and creativity, the importance of mythic structure and the insight available in child-centered communities for healing trauma and grief. A careful exploration of the literature concerning neuro-biology, mythic stories, childhood grief and trauma coupled with qualitative research uncovers a crucible of truth that children do in fact have insights about healing human vulnerability by embracing the genuine nature of deeper interdependent realities.

Children in trauma

As world communities become more impacted by the unpredictability of terrorist attacks and natural disasters, such as the events of 11 September 2001 in the United States, the train explosions in Madrid on 11 March 2004, the London bombings of 7 July 2005, the ongoing conflict in Palestine, Israel, Lebanon, Ireland, the Sudan, Somalia, Darfur, Afghanistan, and Iraq, the tsunami in South East Asia, Hurricane Katrina in the Gulf Coast of the United States, to name a few, people's perceptions of reality have been reshaped due to the imminence of conflict, loss and terror. With the raising of the terror alert to orange in the United States and the immediacy of news events from around the world, fear of death and loss has become the norm. However, for millions of refugees, immigrants and families from war-torn countries and those affected directly by terrorist events, experiences of war, dismemberment, death and chaos are so profound that their reality is life in a constant state of fear.

Children within these families face unspeakable loss with few outlets or resources to deal with the pain. For them and for all the children and adults who interact in their community, the challenge is to join their tragedy in a way that both recognizes the truth of their experience, gives witness to their pain, and develops a basic trust and safety that allows hope to emerge through their exploration and through their self-healing.

The aim of this book is to demonstrate that traumatized children have the potential to lead the healing process. This book shows that through interpersonal relationships and action-centered activities children are able to undertake this course of action, and explores the healing potential of play, creativity, expression and an appreciation and exploration of myth.

The power of play

One of the ways in which children are able to manage trauma is through play. Free play is fundamental to human development. Childhood play is the best opportunity that humanity has to offer our children. It is through play that children wrestle with the emotional and intellectual challenges they encounter. Children with any childhood abilities left within them will play at what they know. Children naturally move in and out of grief due to their development. Children who are refugees and live in war-torn countries learn extreme survival skills. Unlike Post Traumatic Stress Disorder (PTSD), where people want to get away from the events and its triggers, some of the more catastrophic losses are impossible to get away from. Refugees are faced with traumatic bereavement which is a direct assault on the order of their familial and cultural lives and therefore impossible to escape.

Children who are psychically injured, go directly to their inner selves and to their inner voice of imagination when support is provided. By finding new possibilities in exploring old experiences and creating new outcomes children access the ability to grow through grief. Somehow basic assumptions and myths about life have been challenged, stressed and sometimes obliterated. This imaginative capacity is a necessary component for healing with children as well as adults. Finding inner stories and creative expressions allows conquest of their worst fears and feelings. Such processes result in the reconstruction of meaning and discovering the deeper lessons in tragedy.

Trusting this deeper exploration and building a safe relationship with children has become pivotal to moving inside for answers.

Children are open to the silent deeper truths of human survival. Interwoven in the matrix of nature, creativity, and magic, children form a total and believable relationship between themselves, their life lessons and the process of making meaning out of these realities through ritual, play, and the free spontaneous use of art materials. Stories that they create are both awesome and archetypal in their ability to transcend conscious structures and to join the more unfettered reality of unconscious order, meaning and insight. Resilient by nature, children dare to make personal contact with nature, with feelings and with their imaginative abilities. The animistic quality inherent in children's play allows them the opportunity to attribute aspects of their own unconscious life to nature as a whole or to animate and inanimate objects and images. The opportunity for memories to arise happens spontaneously in their play through their humor, with their artistic expression, through their social interactions and interpersonal relationships.

Utilizing these action and art-centered activities children are able to find authentic voice and are capable of transcending otherwise insurmountable realities. What is even more significant about these activities is that they are driven by the child's instinct. By determining the agenda they take a central role in the healing process. In other words, it is important to recognize and respect the child's wisdom and spirited ability to play with the joyful and painful aspects of their life.

The power of myth and stories

Change and the human capacity to transform and integrate trauma and misfortune is directly mediated by the human instinct to embrace humanity, to be creative and to see the possibility of hope and change. Throughout the ages mankind has turned to art, poetry, writing, music, drama and the like not merely to record the reality of their struggle but to reassert the need to uncover meaning and to fight back with the most powerful gift: to be human. In a world where conflict is a common term at the local and global level, communities need to rediscover the power and magnitude of the creative human spirit.

Well documented in art history, in world myths, in legends, in literature, in theology and in the arts, are the compelling images and stories about how mankind and the natural world have co-existed. Human survival and the struggle to find meaning in the face of adversity have interfaced with each other and with nature throughout these compelling stories and images. Rediscovering the underlying ability to survive is a task given to the visionary, the prophet, the savior, the shaman, the wizard. Within an historic and more contemporary framework, the heroines and heroes have often been the common person. Stories that have relevance often bear a universal and humanitarian theme that emerges from the common person's failures and successes. The struggle between good and evil gives way to humane efforts and insights gained only by trial and tribulation. Over and over again the frail and human spirit succumbs to the joys and sadness of the mundane and sometimes tragic forces in everyday life.

We have provided some examples below of common stories and myths which offer illuminating insights into the nature of trauma.

Exerted from Stern in *The Complete Grimm's Fairy Tales* (1972), the stories of Cinderella and Hansel and Gretel illustrate that the simplest insights and personal victories occur whilst the suffering is most intense and the possibility of hope seems nearly impossible. The Brothers Grimm forge the reader forward in their compelling tales which masterfully play with the forces of power, nature and mankind.

When Cinderella's father happened to go to a fair he asked his two step-daughters and Cinderella what he should bring back for them. "Beautiful dresses," said one, "Pearls and jewels," said the second and Cinderella asked her father to break off the first branch which hits his hat on the way home. Cinderella thanks her father and takes the hazel twig to her mother's grave and plants it. Weeping upon every visit to her mother's grave, Cinderella's tears water the twig which grows into a handsome tree. Three times a day Cinderella goes and sits beneath the tree weeping and praying. Soon she is aware of a white bird visiting the tree whenever she sits beneath it. And if Cinderella expresses a wish, the bird throws down to her whatever she wishes for. Cinderella's stepmother throws lentils into the ashes and proclaims that if Cinderella is able to retrieve the lentils within two hours then she may go to the king's wedding festival where the king's son will select a bride.

Cinderella goes directly to the garden and beckons for help from all the birds beneath the sky. No matter how many times the stepmother throws the lentils into the ashes the birds quickly recover them. However, she still protests to Cinderella that she is without dress and shoes and therefore cannot go. Cinderella retreats to the hazel tree at her mother's grave and cries: "Shiver and quiver, little tree, silver and gold throw down over me."

Cinderella receives a gold and silver embroidered silk dress and slippers. She puts on the dress and slippers and quickly goes to the wedding festival. Although we all know what happens next it is remarkable that through Cinderella's suffering comes the nest of her own healing. She builds the safety and security within herself and in her rituals at her mother's grave in order to create a remarkable transformation.

In the tale of Hansel and Gretel a brother and sister are taken into the deep woods by their parents. Their evil stepmother insists that they should be left in order that she and her husband may survive a great dearth that has left them without food and sustenance. The father's heart is heavy but the stepmother insists on the mission to get rid of their children.

Overhearing the stepmother's plan Hansel is wise and collects white pebbles the night before that can be seen in the moonlight in order to find his way back home. Together Hansel and Gretel return to their home after being abandoned in the forest. After a short stay at home, food again becomes scarce and the mad woman takes the children back into the forest by herself. Hansel was unable to get white pebbles because the night before their departure the door was locked. Instead he takes his last piece of bread and drops bread crumbs along the path.

The bread crumbs are eaten by the birds so the children wander deeper into the forest. A snow-white bird sings a delightful song, and then leads the children to an enchanted house "built of bread and covered with cakes." Eating the delectable treats, the children are frightened by the sudden appearance of an ancient woman on crutches. She invites them into her house and feeds them well and then puts them to bed. Hansel and Gretel lie down believing that they are in heaven.

The old woman had only pretended to be so kind. In reality she was a wicked witch, who lay in wait for children and had only built the little house of bread and cake in order to entice them.

Whenever children fell into her power, she would seduce them, she would kill them and then cook them for food. The witch locks Hansel into a stable and feeds him in order to get him fat for cooking. Gretel becomes aware of their plight. The witch tries to get Gretel into the oven. However, Gretel complains about not fitting and as the witch demonstrates by putting her own head in, Gretel pushes her in and fastens the door.

Hansel and Gretel escape with the witch's pearls and jewels. Needing passage across the river they speak to a duck who carries them one by one across the water. As the forest becomes more and more familiar, they soon find their father's house. Their father had not been happy since their departure. The evil woman had died. All their anxiety had ended. Again from within themselves and from within the resources of nature come all the necessary gifts in navigating through the forest and in ultimately discovering their path to freedom, health and well-being.

In a collection of Chinese fairy tales by Lau (1978), The Queen of Tung Ting Lake illustrates the story of Chen who was an ambitious young man of great intelligence. His family was too poor to help him become a scholar, so he instead became the secretary of a famous general who ruled Peking. One day while crossing Tung Ting Lake aboard a junk, the general sights a seal and spears it only for the practice of sportsmanship. Tying the seal to the foot of the mast, Chen and other sailors notice a small fish is attached to the seal's tail. Even out of the water the small fish stays attached.

The general goes to bed pleased with his catch for the day. Chen who stays on deck feels empathy for the seal and uses some healing powder to heal its wounds. Untying the seal he releases the seal and fish connected to it back into the great lake. The seal happily jumps in and out of the water almost in display of its appreciation. Nearby a school of shining fishes, some similar to the one that gripped the seal's tail, join the seal and together they swim away.

The general was not upset that the seal was gone, because it was the hunt and conquest that gave him pleasure, not the victim itself. A year later crossing the same lake a huge storm arises, destroying the junk that Chen is in. Clinging to a bamboo basket, Chen manages to reach the nearby shore where he holds on to tree roots and finally crawls up an embankment to safety. Ravaged by the storm, Chen waits until dawn and then stumbles up a green sloping hill in order to find help and a way back to his native village.

Suddenly an arrow passes by his head. Chen turns to see two beautiful maidens passing by on strong and swift horses. The landscape is beautiful and they are dressed in dresses of purple, with green sashes and red silk holding back their black long hair. Taking cover Chen soon reaches a plateau where he sees many of the young women in hunting costume, laughing, dancing and playing hide and seek within the landscape of lush willow trees, walnut trees and bushes.

Still hiding, Chen soon discovers that the only males there are boys who are serving drinks and refreshments. When one of the boys comes near where he is hiding, Chen quickly gets his attention. He tells the boy about the storm and that his junk has sunk. Desperately he asks of his whereabouts and explains how he is hungry, thirsty and lost. The boy offers him the food and drink that he carries, explains that he is in the hunting ground of Queen Tung Ting and that if he values his life he should leave at once before the queen sees him.

One thing leads to another and Chen goes through a walled gateway into enchanted gardens. Maidens swing in a swing that is hung from the clouds and goes into the sky. Finding a red scarf and a pearl-inlaid writing table, Chen writes a poem about the beautiful princess who rose on the swing into the heavens.

Being discovered in the garden he is asked to stay put. Fearful, he does what is asked of him. Returning the red scarf to the maiden who finds him, he is told that the queen will be summoned. The next morning he is given breakfast, yet the maiden fears for his life because the queen had heard about his writing on the red scarf. Chen pleads for her help finding his way home but also now fears for his life. A team of men with chains move toward him and just as they surround him, the princess that he has observed on the swing moves forward and asks him if he is Lord Chen. He replies "yes" and she tells the men to stop until she has spoken to her mother, the queen. Chen is then taken to the queen's chamber. Begging to be set free and to find his way home, Chen pays honor to the queen.

The queen then thanks him for saving her life and asks him to forgive her for the way that he has been treated and explains that her daughter whose scarf he found and wrote on would be honored to become his wife. A banquet is prepared and Chen knows that he is fortunate and has every reason to celebrate.

Chen's wife describes how her mother, the queen of the lake, can shape-change and how the Queen of Tung Ting Lake was the seal that had been speared. The fish attached to the tail was in fact she and they both thanked him for saving their lives that night on the junk.

In this Chinese fairy tale, Chen finds himself on a journey not of his choosing. As a result of the storm at sea he has struggled for his life, leaving his identity of poverty and servitude behind. What is most impressive is that the story portrays several realities. The nature of Tung Ting Lake, the conscious life of Chen and a symbolic reality whereby his act of kindness actually affects a larger, more spiritual realm, helping to reinforce a notion of the interconnection between human kind, nature and larger realities. In the land of Queen Tung Ting, life is sensual by nature. Women are the dominant figures who ride horseback and live in a beauteous relationship between themselves and the natural world. Swings drop from the clouds, Queen Tung Ting can shape-shift herself into a seal or other natural forms, life is sensual and free flowing. The reversal of women leading and men in a supportive roles heightens the attention to a more feminine, nature-centered reality.

Chen accepts the celebration and feels honored and gifted to find such a beautiful bride. Once he is able to let go of his need to find his way back to his previous reality, he understands the truth of his connection to Queen Tung Ting and her beautiful daughter.

At the end of the tale, Chen and his princess bride were afloat in their beautiful hand-carved, pearl-inlaid junk with scarlet shutters and floral wreathes. Suddenly mandarin Liang who was Chen's closet boyhood friend, happened by in his own junk. He got close enough to recognize Chen's face. Chen ordered his junk to stop and invited Liang aboard to meet his wife.

Liang could not imagine how this penniless student had managed to become so wealthy and married to such a beautiful and elegant lady. When the servants presented wonderful food on gold and diamond-inlaid plates, he could no longer hold back his curiosity. Liang then asserted that when he had seen Chen ten years ago he was a poor man.

Chen laughed and agreed and discovered that Liang had been south for the last ten years. This was his first time returning home. Chen declared that since he hadn't been home for ten years then he was unaware of the changes in Chen's life. Upon leaving, Chen gives Liang a beautiful pearl as a token of their visit. When arriving at Chen's native village, Liang asks friends about the news of their friend Chen. When he tells them that Chen is extremely wealthy and has a beautiful wife, his friends are aghast and claim that Liang has made a great mistake.

According to the friends from the village, Chen was a secretary to a general. He was coming home for vacation and crossing Tung Ting Lake when his junk sank in a terrible storm. He drowned and was never recovered. Chen has been dead for years. Liang was amazed and never found an explanation for his strange meeting with Chen. He passed the beautiful, priceless pearl down from one generation to the next. The pearl was his only reminder of his mysterious encounter.

This tale leaves the reader with many unanswered questions. Speaking of realms unknown, the tale captures both a conscious and a dream-like quality. Whatever its intention the tale illustrates how Chen is led to his greatest wish by being open to mysterious, deeper realities. Throughout his own quest for life and meaning he progresses not by wealth but by good deeds which are natural to his inner being. He becomes more wealthy and gifted by being truly who he is. The pearl becomes a symbol of both the mystery and the beauty of engaging in connections that lay beyond his control.

Abstracted from the tales of the Thousand and One Nights, and Arabian Nights, Ludmila Zeman (1999) tells the enchanted tale of Sindbad the Sailor As the story starts Shahangad who is a young and beautiful woman introduces herself to a wicked king who beheads his wives one after another in pursuit of his own desires and happiness. She believes that she can end the king's "wicked ways" by telling him one tale after another giving him little time for rest or evil behavior. For a thousand and one nights, Shahangad accomplishes her mission. The king is spellbound by her story telling and orders his craftsman to "weave her beautiful stories into the finest carpets."

The story of Sindbad the sailor starts in the city of Baghdad. A poor laboring porter by the name of Sindbad passes through the streets of Baghdad with a heavy load on his back. As he struggles under such labor a handsome old man passes who shows great wealth. He is riding a large elephant with tapestries, silk and elegant canopy above his head. His servants wave their ornate feathered fans and call this royal man Sindbad. Reflecting to himself on the contrast between his plight as a poor porter and carrying such a heavy load on his back, Sindbad feels the misery of his position in contrast to the great wealth and prestige of the wealthy Sindbad who has such good fortune.

Unbeknown to him, the wealthy Sindbad has overheard his lament and beckons to his servant to get the attention of the poor porter and bring him to his palace. Reluctant at first the porter fears that the master will punish him for such lamentation. Finally he accompanies the servant to the grand palace filled with refined and magnificent beauty. The master implores the porter to sit and to eat all that he might desire. He then goes on to say how curious it is that their names are the same yet their calling in life is different. The master goes on to say that he too has known poverty, hunger, thirst and great danger. The master then tells Sindbad the story of his great wealth and great loss.

His father was the wealthiest merchant in the city of Baghdad. When Sindbad's father died he had inherited all of his wealth and many estates and possessions. However, due to his lavish life style he wasted his wealth and good fortune. It wasn't long before he became a pauper. He decided to become a sailor on a merchant ship and sailed from Baghdad down the Tigres river to the Persian Gulf, the Arabian sea and to great oceans beyond. He actually became fond of his new adventurous life and of all the foreign lands and people that he encountered. He tried to learn what he could about the cultures, traditions and languages in these new lands.

One day as he traveled on his sea-faring adventures, Sindbad and his fellow sailors happened upon an island as lush and beautiful as a virtual garden of Eden. All seemed well, Sindbad and his mates had all rushed ashore to prepare a feast and to explore the island. Sindbad found some giant coconut palms. He was just about to split one open with his dagger when his knife went through the coconut and into the ground. Much to his surprise blood rose into the air and the whole island moved as if the sea was engulfing it with all its strength.

The captain who had stayed on the ship screamed to the sailors to run for their lives. What had seemed like an island was in fact a giant whale who had floated long enough to get an actual growth of trees and life on its back. The waves and sea overwhelmed everyone. Sindbad grasped for a wooden barrel floating by and hung on for dear life. He could not reach the ship. Sindbad had just about given up hope when he saw an island with smooth sands and a huge white mountain on it.

Each step of the journey, Sindbad is resilient in his ability to let go of one reality, enter another and find his way toward freedom. The strange island has a giant bird that lays a white egg the size of a mountain. When Sindbad ties himself to the bird's talons, he is dropped into a pit of deadly snakes. What is more mysterious is that this pit is also covered with great diamonds and jewels.

The tale continues to play with the metaphors of the good and the bad, the strong and the weak, the rich and the poor, the loss and the gain of power and control over his own life. What is remarkable is that the tale demonstrates the forces in life which often take us to places that we are not prepared to go.

His journey and ultimate transformation takes place in a highly imaginative realm that teaches both the geographic and material richness of this land where human life began. Mesopotamia, the garden of Eden and the wealth of the worldly treasures are captured in these tales. Sindbad plays with reality through his own transformation. His telling of his tale to a poor porter underscores the notion that what seems impossible about their connections becomes enlightened and visible as the tale unfolds. One is transported from the personal realm to a more spiritual realm, from the local experience to the non-local and from a sense of control to a sense of transformation.

Ultimately the tale of Sindbad the Sailor takes the reader into the deeper realms of making connections with dark, adventurous often unknown elements of life that help us to better understand our fate as well as our vulnerability of being human but somehow connected to a larger picture that we don't always understand. The outer world acts as a mirror, reflecting on the many inner parts of ourselves that ultimately can be integrated through illumination.

The examples above illustrate how mythical realities reveal an underlying more unconscious structure of a world un-molded by conscious reality.

Children have an autotelic nature in understanding and believing in the reality of the animistic nature of life. At a deeper level there is no separation between the conscious and unconscious world. The unconscious both in dreams and free play acts as a direct language for the active creation of inner order when the outer world has presented trauma and chaos. Psychic entropy and the need for regaining inner harmony is mediated only by the creative human spirit.

Children have an intrinsic ability to play with the inner connections between themselves, the events in their life and the natural and imaginative kingdom. New order emerges when children are capable of playing with disorder, chaos and ultimately the traumatic events that have shaped their life. Fairy tale structure is frequently a choice that children draw from in order to replay their own misfortunes and to develop new outcomes that help change their perceptions of themselves and of the world. Embedded within the structure of fairy tales is the ability to face paradoxical realities. Bad people and events can spontaneously turn into opportunities for discovery and change. What at first may seem like a disconnected event or circumstance may actually be good fortune.

Mythic structure has a universal appeal to children and adults alike. In clinical work children who are faced with the unspeakable tragedy of medical disease, foster care, the loss of parents and family, divorce, physical injury and other traumatic events will turn to fairy tales as a means of working out the complex path to wellness. Cinderella, Hansel and Gretel,

Snow White, Little Red Riding Hood, Sleeping Beauty, Rumpelstiltskin, are but a few of the tales that get reconfigured into the personal tragedy and events surrounding children's grief. The energy of the ugly witch, the ugly stepmother, the good or evil queen, compassionate fairies, magical wizard, enchanted sprite, lost princess, challenged prince, all come into action as the various parts of children's life stories seek expression and resolution. Scenes are played out with personal attention to specific re-enactments. Over and over again children repeat patterns such as finding the lost princess, the queen who is unable to see her daughter's beauty or the movement between the royal home and the witch's cottage, symbolic of the movement between the foster home and the child's home of origin. This playful activity portrays the truthful nature of the inner life. Whatever the sources of trauma and grief, children have the ability to both comprehend and resolve life's difficulties by playing out all parts of themselves and the story and searching for personal and collective truth.

Working with children

Because children will naturally seek an imaginative course of exploration and play when they feel supported and reassured, facilitators are challenged by the action and metaphors that such play generates.

Imagination and human stories are key forces in opening pathways toward integrating and organizing the highly complex realities of trauma. The power of the unconscious represents the new frontier in human potentiality. As we play with the interconnection between feelings and rational thoughts we harness the potential for re-ordering personal and collective perceptions of reality. Inner peace, harmony and the collective need for beauty and creativity are the caldron and wellspring for justice and humane understanding and expression.

Within clinical work with children and work with children in communities certain common forces co-exist. A primary need to re-establish trust and safety is elemental to trauma recovery. Once the trust is established children need to be supported to be spontaneous. Spontaneity in art, play, drama, provide the support to move toward self-disclosure. The relationship between children and their adult facilitators needs to be based on honesty, acceptance, safety and openness. Trust is earned. Trust is not an automatic entity but a quality that builds within a relationship based on an ongoing belief that healing is instinctive and that a path to wellness is not outer directed but inner generated.

Just when trust has been established the chance for more personal, auto-biographical or uncensored unconscious material to arise becomes possible. What cannot be predicted is the content both emotional and cognitive. Spontaneity opens the door for creative ability as well as affective expression.

Anger, fear, conflict and anxiety may become visible and palpable in the creative process as well as within the relationship itself. Art materials and games often become the active hands-on connection to this process. This is a time in individual as well as community work when the limits, rules and purposes get questioned. A guiding principle is that conflict is necessary for development to occur. It's also a point in multicultural group work when dominant cultural requirements are questioned and challenged.

Ambivalence actually exists throughout a creative unfolding. Just when trust seems permanent it gets tested again. Just when the emotional content seems highest, it re-occurs with new and unprecedented intensity. Just when new understandings and integrations occur other realities emerge. In work within multicultural groups the culture of origin and the dominant culture become concepts that are conflictual and at times separate and intolerable.

Children's creative expressions and verbal content regarding past trauma and loss become more visible as the process allows for the past, present and future to be visited and more openly interwoven. In multicultural groups there is more openness about sharing the rituals, losses and experiences in the culture of origin as well as exploring the rituals, losses and experiences within the dominant culture. Thoughts and fantasies about the future become both tolerable and hopeful as the past and present become more integrated.

Letting go, children in individual work as well as community groups become better able to be in the moment and less blocked by primary or secondary defenses such as denial and avoidance. The personal need for control and the hesitancy to engage in spontaneous experience is replaced by more frequent and genuine creative expressions and open dialogue. At this point the communication, the relationship, as well as the creative process is more generative. New connections and insights are being made between the creative material and dialogue and the new meaning attached to these expressions.

Hopefulness and more positive affect is associated with the end phase of individual and community work. There is a level of maturation that has occurred both through the relationships and through the creative expression. At this phase in the process change is observable and becomes internally integrated. There often is more positive reference to the future and children have often successfully shed some of the underlying anger, conflict, fear and anxiety. Possibilities for change and transformation are available. At this point in the process, rituals, images and stories that have been repeated, change, transform or shift into new integrated forms.

Following is a diagram (Figure 0.1) that looks at the developmental framework in this peer support, community-based, change process. The process is not linear but in fact is curvilinear. Like the game of snakes and ladders surprises are the norm. Any one phase may be repeated whenever necessary in order to gain the stability and balance to move forward. The progression of the table illustrates the developmental progression as well as the close inter-relationship between the various phases. The left-hand column further identifies each phase in the process and the right-hand column is a parallel description of similiar qualities found in myth literature.

References

Lau, J. (1978) *Traditional Chinese Stories*. New York: Columbia University Press.

Stern, J. (1972) *The Complete Grimm's Fairy Tales*. New York: Pantheon Books.

Zeman, L. (1999) *Sindbad: From the Tales of the Thousand and One Nights*. Toronto: Tundra Books.

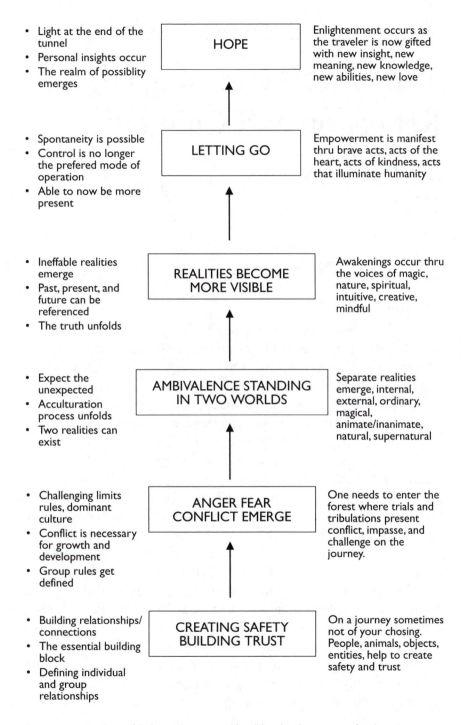

- Light at the end of the tunnel
- Personal insights occur
- The realm of possiblity emerges

HOPE

Enlightenment occurs as the traveler is now gifted with new insight, new meaning, new knowledge, new abilities, new love

- Spontaneity is possible
- Control is no longer the prefered mode of operation
- Able to now be more present

LETTING GO

Empowerment is manifest thru brave acts, acts of the heart, acts of kindness, acts that illuminate humanity

- Ineffable realities emerge
- Past, present, and future can be referenced
- The truth unfolds

REALITIES BECOME MORE VISIBLE

Awakenings occur thru the voices of magic, nature, spiritual, intuitive, creative, mindful

- Expect the unexpected
- Acculturation process unfolds
- Two realities can exist

AMBIVALENCE STANDING IN TWO WORLDS

Separate realities emerge, internal, external, ordinary, magical, animate/inanimate, natural, supernatural

- Challenging limits rules, dominant culture
- Conflict is necessary for growth and development
- Group rules get defined

ANGER FEAR CONFLICT EMERGE

One needs to enter the forest where trials and tribulations present conflict, impasse, and challenge on the journey.

- Building relationships/ connections
- The essential building block
- Defining individual and group relationships

CREATING SAFETY BUILDING TRUST

On a journey sometimes not of your chosing. People, animals, objects, entities, help to create safety and trust

Figure 0.1 Group phases of dealing with trauma and loss (likened to the structures of myths and games there are frequent shifts back and forth between stages)

CHAPTER 1

The Importance of Myth, Reflection and Cultural Sensitivity

Introduction

Deeply embedded within each person's life story are essential truths like those found in fairy tales and myth structures. The path that needs to be followed, the life lessons that need to be integrated and learned and the ultimate truth about our human limits and possibilities are held within a personal, internal realm. Autobiographical by nature, humankind wishes to be heard and more importantly to be understood. Personal encounters with trauma and loss create more complexity and confusion.

The human attributes of empathy, love and creativity are the essential supports and building blocks toward expressing complicated truths. Not knowing is often a point of struggle for both the traumatized client and the facilitator in the process. Discovering new connections between traumatic experiences and the feelings as well as physical sensations associated with such events means developing a safe place and safe relationship where such complex truths can be explored without being repeated.

Following are moments in a highly evolved creative and relational process whereby children bring the truth to light. Heroic by nature is the fact that such truths are both expressed and ameliorated in a natural way. Enlightenment is slow and at times unavailable when there is no opportunity for reflection or overview. Captured over time, stories, images, personal and social interactions and actual changes in the personal perception and awareness represent the springboard to insight, reflection and integration.

Grief and trauma literature, concepts of mythic structures, neuro-research and actual personal, social and creative encounters illustrate further the significance of self-healing. Awakening to the truth readers will discover that personal, social and cultural perceptions interact with uniquely held mythic truths about how the world operates. Personal myths are inseparable from collective myths. What is unique is that supporting the expression of inner truths opens the door for complex inquiry. For a time when quick answers, speedy cures, instantaneous computerized information and simple theories are sought after, this book theorizes that true solace for the trauma and loss in contemporary times is not simple. Instead such times require entry into the complex inner realities of personal and collective myths. Trust and meaningful personal relationships coupled with creative exploration open the door where the opportunity arises to both express and integrate emotions, experiences and sensations thereby uncovering the healing path to recovery.

Deepening trust

The child develops perceptions of the world both based on their direct encounters with culture which includes early and formative relationships. A multiply complex matrix between personal life experience, interpersonal, social, cultural, spiritual and developmental realities form a basis of individual perception. Such complexities not only form the basis of identity, but also establish the ways in which one interacts with the outside world. Based on the aforementioned, we believe that the concept of multicultural competence is flawed. It is a myth to assume that even with an academic understanding of different cultures, assumptions can be made concerning individuals and their family beliefs. Furthermore, even within one's own culture the highly specific beliefs and myths held within a particular family, community or individual may be hidden and virtually unexplored. Complicating such intricate complexity is the impact of trauma and loss. During such encounters adults as well as children experience chaos and upheaval of previously held beliefs. Searching for the truth and needing to resolve conflict results in an uprising and battle with one's self. Sorting through the realm of possibilities results in a highly individualized integration between the pain and suffering and the meaning of one's life.

We question the notion that one can become "competent" at the culture of another as well as the experiences of another (Goldberg 2000). We would instead propose a model in which building trust and maintaining awareness is the goal for establishing competence. With "lack of competence" as the focus, a different view of practicing across culture emerges. The child is the "expert" and the facilitator is in a position of seeking knowledge and trying to understand what life is like for the child. There is no thought of competence—instead one thinks of gaining understanding (always partial) of a phenomenon that is evolving and changing. Unfortunately, most of us are ill prepared for this role. Helping professionals have been trained by those who taught about theories and techniques developed within their own cultural context. There is an irony here that as the world shrinks one becomes more aware of other cultures. Yet, as nations become more culturally mixed, it is more difficult to separate out the contributions of cultural differences.

In an ideal world most people would know about different cultures, be they regional, national, racial, religious, disability or gender oriented, or any combination. People would also adjust their behavior accordingly. However, in reality people are mortals who are neither infinitely flexible nor infinitely wise.

Rather than trying to fit children into formulas, we believe we should let them tell us about themselves through their art, their body language, their emotions and their words. Cultural specific therapeutic traditions are replete with instances in which legitimate subcultural expressions are pathologized, marginalized, or misinterpreted. This tendency toward monocultural universalism has undermined the complexity of diverse cultural traditions. However, art, play, story telling and other creative, spontaneous outlets have the unique opportunity to depart from this heritage by serving as a means for diverse cultural expression and enrichment.

Art itself may have different conceptions and functions in other cultures. Compare, for instance, writing as an art form in Asian cultures, design as a highly developed ability in Islamic cultures, or the evolved understanding of color and the spiritual function of art in indigenous cultures. The notion that art provides psychological healing in another culture is an assumption and the means by which it may do so is likely to differ from one cultural convention and ritual to another (Acton 2001).

It is critical to stay open to any indigenous or local healing traditions that are essential for cultural integrity and community identity. People need to be consciously aware of how certain individuals continue to force the patterns and rituals of western enculturation and colonization.

Our individualistic concept of the autonomous self may be in contradiction with the interdependent orientation or emphasis on family bonds found with some collectivist cultures (e.g. most Asian cultures) (Pendersen 1988).

Since one's growth and the resolution of problems are rooted in family and community relationships in these cultures, self-exploration and individual decision making may be seen as self-indulgent and a threat to the social matrix. Finding help and assistance within community is natural to Asian cultures (Hocoy 1999).

Children may experience gender, age and development as critical factors. Individuals of Asian, Native American, and Middle Eastern heritage may still uphold gender and age as indicators of status, authority, wisdom and knowledge (Samuda and Wolfgang 1985).

Norms and standards based on a dominant culture have served to pathologize and discriminate against minority individuals as well as justify and perpetuate a social order that privileges those of the dominant culture. Testing and assessment favors individuals from cultures that emphasize field-independent cognitive styles and verbal and analytical abilities rather than field-sensitive cognitive styles that relate well to concepts in humanized or story format, of concepts that relate to personal interests or lived experience (Berry and Bennett 1989). Other characteristics of the field-sensitive cognitive style are the seeking of social rewards to strengthening relationships with others and the seeking of guidance and demonstration from teachers. The field-sensitive style has been found to be characteristic of many minority groups (e.g. Native Americans, Asian and Middle Eastern) (Samuda 1990).

Effective integration of cultural differences

Acculturation is defined as cultural change that results from continuous first-hand contact between two distinct cultural groups (Redfield, Linton and Herskovits 1936).

For individuals of minority backgrounds, issues of cultural identity are commonly found to be important to growth and development (Hocoy 1999). Acculturation speaks to the psychological process of an individual negotiating cross-cultural contact. This involves self-esteem, personal identity, general mental health and attitudes towards oneself, one's cultural group and the dominant group. The prevailing framework of acculturation that accounts for an individual's relationship to the dominant culture and to his or her culture of origin derives from the work of J.W. Berry (1998). The framework describes four models of acculturation (Integration, Assimilation, Separation, and Marginalization). Successful integration is based on an individual's cultural identity maintenance and his or her relationship with the dominant culture. The process involves the maintenance of cultural integrity as well as full participation in the dominant culture. Assimilation results when aspects of one's culture of origin are embraced while identifying with the dominant culture. Separation involves maintaining cultural identity and rejecting the dominant culture. Marginalization involves a loss of identification with either one's culture of origin or the dominant culture (Hocoy 1999).

It is critical to recognize that interpretation is never culture free, that there is always the imposition of a set of meaning structures that derive from a particular cultural context (Greenfield 1997). For example, historically the image of the dragon in many western narratives often embodies evil or the devil; while in many eastern cultures it has always represented an embodiment of the power of the divine or the numinous, the image of which is considered to bring fortune and prosperity (Hocoy 1999). Therefore, a valid cross-cultural interpretation requires the application of a set of meaning structures consistent with the cultural background of the individual whose work is being interpreted.

Given the constraints inherent in cross-cultural interpretation, art and creative expression should emphasize process, experience and personal meanings for the child (Fagan 1998). Artistic expression as a means of amplifying the symbolic level of the child's experience (Koff-Chapin 1996), or his or her intuitive experience (Belanger 1998), may be more effective than one that strives for reliability and accuracy in interpretation.

An understanding of the community in which the families live, its resources (i.e. religious organizations), and the impinging issues of personal violence and social problems is critical for effective intervention (Douglas 1993). An investigation of how art and spontaneous expression is utilized as a means of healing in a child's culture of origin is invaluable (Acton 2001).

In the work of Florence Cane (1983), art therapist, children are encouraged to know the world through thought, movement, feeling and providing an action approach that utilizes many senses and does not rely on a verbal didactic communication. Art becomes a major form of dialogue among children and between the children and the facilitators. Children utilized large easels and large paper with art media in a body-centered approach whereby spontaneous expression led to more expressive possibilites.

Resilient themes are observed through the art and often exhibited in role playing, conversation and body-centered activities.

Despite divergent cultural backgrounds, nearly all refugees encounter similar kinds of resettlement difficulties (Beiser, Turner and Ganesan 1989; Burvill 1973; Cervantes, Salgado and Padilla 1989; Farias 1991). These common stresses of cross-cultural adaptation may be exhibited through unresolved grief, intergenerational conflict and various psychological and behavioral manifestations of distress.

Discovering the meaning of personal and collective stories

Mythic structures are the personal and collective stories of humanity's struggle for meaning. Unaffected by history or time, certain myths and epic writings go directly to the truth of unmitigated pain and the struggle of resolving and healing human trauma. Wisdom through the ages is reflected through the timeless stories told in fairy tales, folklore and through the epic myths of native people from all the world's nations. Unparalleled in its genuine ability to be open to the truth of human suffering and misery is *The Iliad* or the "Poem of Force."

Homer's genius understood at a deep level the unobservable reality of how human fate is directed by the larger forces of nature and mankind. This epic genius uncovers the realities that actually govern human events as well as nature and ultimately provide opportunities for the human soul to express more freely its purpose and mission. Greek heroes and heroines succumb, one by one, to the loss of power and control only to face once again the vulnerable path to ultimate fate. Each episode in the myth uncovers human vulnerability that forces people to no longer administer power, greed, or violence as the prevailing truth that separates the enemy from the victim. Instead heroines and heroes recognize connection rather than alienation from their enemy. Such truths are only uncovered when they exercise the ability to pause and reflect. Stopping as they ponder is the only opportunity to consider hope or future peace.

In *The Iliad* Homer well describes his theme of how violence co-exists with humanity and compassion. Likened to the two symbols emblazoned on Achilles' shield with one city at war and the other city at peace, Homer clearly illustrates through his writing how various heroines and heroes succumb to the tragedy of war and chaos with moments when they have opportunity to imagine otherwise.

Parallel to the theme of this book, within the pain and struggle of trauma and chaos are the seeds for wisdom, insight and ultimate integration and peace.

In a very dark moment when Apollo's priest Chryses confronts the King Agamemnon with his unwillingness to co-operate in order to gain back Chryses' daughter Chryseis, a plague breaks out amongst Agamemnon's soldiers. Apollo the son of Zeus and Leta is incensed by the king's refusal to co-operate. Men die of the plague and yet Agamemnon continues to spurn Apollo's priest and his pleas and ransom for his daughter's safe return. Achilles is called upon to recover Chryseis reminding Agamemnon that he has offended Apollo and that he must return the priest's daughter. Achilles is gripped with an anguishing rage as Agamemnon refuses to follow the will of Apollo. Finally Agamemnon agrees that he will take Chryseis back but that he will send her back with his own ship and with his own crew. In return he tells Achilles that he will take Briseis who is Achilles' beautiful partner. Enraged Achilles was about to draw his blade when the muse Athena was sent down from the heavens by the white goddess Hera.

Athena is present in the moment to check Achilles' rage. She pleads with him to stop the fighting, now. Athena believes that Hera cares for and loves both Achilles and Agamemnon alike. She begs Achilles to lay down his sword. The truth according to Athena is that Achilles will be rewarded one day threefold for any outrage that Agamemnon has transacted. Knowing that if a man obeys the gods they will be quick to hear his prayers, Achilles puts his sword back into its sheath.

Chryseis in all her beauty is put aboard a ship and returned to her homeland. King Agamemnon then sent his aides to Achilles' lodge to take Briseis in exchange. Stricken with grief, Achilles lets the aides witness his loss. Achilles prays to his mother. Hearing his prayer, his mother who is with her father, the Old Man of the Sea, comes to her son's aid in voice and spirit. Achilles reviews the story with his mother. He recalls the battle and how Chryseis had been chosen for Agamemnon. How her father the holy priest of Apollo had offered ransom to win his daughter back. He also related how an old seer who knew the truth of Apollo unleashing the plague upon Agamemnon's troops said that it was a plea for Agamemnon to know the will of Apollo. Yet Agamemnon still resisted.

Later in anger Agamemnon does Apollo's will and makes animal sacrifices and yet takes Archilles' beloved Briseis away. At this point Achilles pleas for his mother to go to Olympus and make an appeal to Zeus. Somehow

Achilles felt sure that his mother could help Zeus support the Trojan cause and recognize how Agamemnon had disgraced Achilles. At last Thetis, Achilles' father, speaks and gives support that he will go directly to Zeus to ask for assistance (Homer 1990).

Throughout this passage from *The Iliad*, larger truths about the personal encounters between Agamemnon and Achilles are mediated by Apollo, Zeus, Athena, Apollo's priest, Chryses, the old seer and other entities that remind the characters that other elements, laws of nature, larger spheres are in action and oversee the ultimate order. Unless Achilles gives himself to the power of Athena, Zeus, Apollo and others, then he continues to be imprisoned by his limited view points.

Stopping, pausing, for a moment allows for something else to emerge, even when such action is outside the realm of Achilles' personal control. Giving up the conscious control and preoccupation with the personal nature of tragedy and chaos means letting something else emerge. The characters in other great forms of art, literature, music, poetry and the like beckon for the moment, the present, to expand, open, somehow create a new vantage point. It is as if the weight of the personal suffering has been lifted momentarily in order to catch a glimpse of some other meaning, some different pathway that may allow such diverse realities to co-exist.

Perhaps the door opens momentarily when the imaginative realm, the creative will, the spiritual content, the possibility of hope and transformation can be exercised. Personal freedom to enter such a domain is often not the first conscious choice and yet such choices are made possible when in the imaginative and creative realms. When Achilles chooses to listen to Athena, when he lets go of the tragedy that he faces and asks for assistance from Zeus, when Cinderella beckons for help from the birds, when Hansel and Gretel follow the snow-white bird to the witch's cottage, there is a pause from the personal plight to the collective reality. In such moments the mythic characters move from a position of isolation to inclusion, no longer seeing the separation between the victim and the heroine, between good and evil, between control and freedom.

Simone Weil, a scholar and an activist during the 1920s and early 1930s, associated herself closely with the European poor working-class people in order to share in their trials of conflict and trauma. She personally engaged in the struggles that Parisian factory workers faced with the encroachment of modern technology and mechanization. She was highly involved in the human suffering and racism, along with the cruelties inflicted by the rise to power of the totalitarian regime of Nazi Germany. In 1942 she traveled to the United States with her family as the result of losing her academic post due to imposed racist laws. Anxious to resume her activism she returned to France under war-time conditions. Because of her ongoing struggles with illness, she succumbed in her winter crossing of the Atlantic Ocean and never recovered. Dying prematurely at the age of 34, her life remains a model of humble, empathic wisdom and awareness. She believed in becoming personally affected by and personally supportive to the human suffering and struggles that surrounded her.

Intellectually and emotionally gifted, Simone Weil explored and identified with the highest works and writings of art and science in order to better understand and appreciate the human necessities of suffering and pain. She was the premiere analyst of Homer's Greek tragedy in the *Iliad or the Poem of Force*, and believed that the genius quality of Homer's *Iliad* was to uncover the embedded truth about how no one is superior to human suffering and to human pain and misery. More profound is *The Iliad*'s uncanny ability to create insight about the importance of human complexity and vulnerability as the entrance to insights and healing.

The transformative effect of reflection

Exploring *The Iliad*, Simone Weil points out that "force is that x that turns anybody who is subjected to it into a thing" (Weil 1991, p.3). Illustrations from *The Iliad* describe heroes and heroines being subjected to forces that ultimately take their human life. She goes on to point out that "the most devastating force is the force that does not kill but hangs poised and ready over the person that it could kill at any moment" (Weil 1991, p.4). Accordingly, the ability to turn a human being into a thing while still alive is more anguishing than to die suddenly of a mortal wound. Her apt description of human trauma is as relevant today as it was in this Greek tragedy. Weil points out that when human beings are subjected to the touch or sight of events that are horrible or terrifying that internally "their muscles, nerves and flesh responds" (Weil 1991, p.6).

Forced into silence, the event itself passes but the sensory memory is embedded in the body forever. There is no escape, only the constant need never to return to the event or the feelings associated with it. Vigilance keeps the person protected but the body and soul longs for release, exposure, and some safe event that will purge the "thing" to feel again. Weil describes this well in her synopsis that "their days hold no pastimes, no free spaces, no room in them for any impulse of their own" (Weil 1991, p.8).

Weil believes that mankind, by the act of being born, is destined to suffer violence. The strong are never absolutely strong and the weak are never absolutely weak. Yet both deny that they have anything to do with each other. With little room to interpose between the impulse and the act, neither the strong nor the weak have a moment for reflection. Where there is no room for reflection, there is none either for justice or prudence. The powerful wield their power with no suspicion that there could be consequences to their deeds. Fate often brings the consequences home for them to bear. Often the balance of power is that chance opens them to misfortune.

With no protection, the armor is gone and nothing shields them from the tears and loss. This retribution which has a geometrical rigor operates automatically to penalize the abuse of force. What goes around comes around. No one escapes the consequences of the abusive use of force.

Weil recounts that throughout history and literature mankind is often portrayed as omnipotent. "For they do not see the force in their possession is only a limited quantity; nor do they see their relations with other human beings as a kind of balance between unequal amounts of force. Since other people do not impose on their movements that halt, that internal hesitation, wherein lies all our consideration for our brothers in humanity, they conclude that destiny has given complete licence to them, and none at all to their inferiors" (Weil 1991, p.14).

Weil goes on to point out that in nature force is limited. "Sometimes chance is kind and sometimes cruel" (Weil 1985, p.15) Geometrically the measure of balance has ultimate control. Greeks believed in an unspoken balance in nature as well as in human life. Nemesis became the term describing the central force in Greek tragedies. Karma would be the Buddhist, oriental equivalent notion of nemesis. Weil believed that "violence obliterates anybody who feels its touch. Once you acknowledge death to be a practical possibility, the thought of it becomes unendurable except in flashes" (Weil 1991, pp.21–22).

Providing the sufferer with the resources, which might serve to extricate the pain, means being as willing as Simone Weil was to enter the reality of what those moments humanly and spiritually mean. *The Iliad*, in its use of similes, likens the wound either to "fire, flood, wind, wild beasts or God knows what blind cause of disaster, or else to frightened animals, trees, water, sand, to anything in nature that is set into motion by the violence of external forces" (Weil 1991, p.26).

Simone Weil talks about the conqueror who knows no respect, the despair of the soldier who meets his own destruction, the obliteration of the slave and the many faces of honor revealed in *The Iliad*. Throughout these plights force is the only hero. Yet there are a few moments when reflection, courage, love bring the heroine and heroes toward an inner deliberation, an inner reflection on something soulful. Although such moments of grace are rare in *The Iliad*, they bespeak the ability to separate from the force and therefore the capacity for love and human justice.

Trauma and neuro-biology

As human beings, we try to hold ourselves above or outside the reality of our suffering and pain. With our intellectual and primary defenses of denial, displacement, repression, regression and intellectualization we try to hold back the pain and create a simple reality that sees only what we wish to feel. Yet our human encounters with pain are much more complex and much more body-centered. Simone Weil reminds us in her writing that we are as vulnerable as the characters in *The Iliad* to the forces that shape and impact our lives. No one is spared and yet everyone needs to discover meaning in order to transform themselves into the true purpose or reasons for their life existence.

Simone Weil believes that a deeper connection to the moments themselves, whether tragic or loving, opens the doors for reflection and transformation. Reflection is our only hope for connections to humanity and for the new creation of deeper, more personal myths that support us to discover who we truly are. Creating personal myths, stories, rituals, spontaneous expressions through art, drama, action and play hold the door open for moments of reflection on the deeper meaning, purpose, and choices that we have to know why we are here and to gain insights as to the meaning of our human pain and suffering.

Without reflection there is no opportunity to either release or make connections to the feelings that are stored within our own bodies. This book is charged with moments of reflection. Those moments where children, peers and adults have the opportunity to freely express, spontaneously explore, openly share parts and pieces of their own stories is when opportunity emerges. These transformative opportunities open the door for the deeper connections to their culture of origin, to the often troubled traumatic past, to the war-torn stories of themselves and their families' survival, to the new connections, to the imaginative realm, to the new meanings and understandings that weave these reflections into their present life, to their acculturation and to their future potential.

Trauma and loss not only shape who we are but also remind us of the vulnerability of being human. Integration of such fragmenting experiences offers a pathway to hope. In the following images and stories participants and facilitators alike are drawn together often in the face of huge resistance and defense. The more traumatized children are, the less capable they are of being spontaneous, open and trusting of the relationship with peers, facilitators and the creative process. Joining children's resistance requires what Weil so aptly modeled in her own activism and what is so eloquently illustrated in *The Iliad*. The ability to be present in the resistance allows acceptance that leads to trust and potential reflection. Building trust with children who have witnessed horrible tragedies requires faith that something lies beyond their present behavior and resistance. Only when this trust is built do children dare to enter the more creative possibility of releasing stories, affect, images, and playing more openly with whom they are and what they have experienced.

Moments of joy and despair of the past that need to be integrated into the present and future begin to emerge. Non-dualistic by nature no one is removed from pain and suffering. Facilitators as well as the children enter a space that exposes the truth in re-enactments, dramatizations, images, stories and non-verbal awareness that allow reflection and at the same time challenges the need for connection, understanding and human compassion.

From *The Iliad* to contemporary research on the neuro-biological nature of trauma we can observe certain parallels. Dr. Bessel Van der Kolk, director of the Boston Trauma Center, has published 100 scientific papers including books on traumatic stress and believes that while people who have been traumatized may appear well on the surface, underneath they complain of flashbacks, dissociative symptoms, re-occurring nightmares, and seemingly little ability to re-connect to their daily lives. Van der Kolk has compiled research based on his findings uncovered by veterans' experiences in World War I, World War II, Vietnam, and his research findings concerning schizophrenic patients and Hurricane Hugo survivors. His pioneering efforts have helped to recognize in trauma victims the diagnosis of Post Traumatic Stress Disorder (PTSD) and have pushed the limits of understanding how the human brain may process and resolve such pain. Van der Kolk believes that human vulnerability and physical helplessness are the number one factors in the development of serious post-traumatic symptoms.

Traumatic memories of this nature, according to Van der Kolk, often result in people being unable to modulate their autonomic arousal. Because there is a feeling of helplessness and lack of physical ability to combat or overcome the trauma, Van der Kolk speculates that physical action might contribute to healing (Sykes Wylie 2004).

Van der Kolk believes that the feeling of powerlessness and the inability to escape or fight back results in the human need to re-establish physical efficacy as a biological organism and a need to re-create a sense of safety. Without the action necessary to reclaim this balance people often develop PTSD. Throughout his writings references are frequently made to the developing brain as being an action organ that evidences the formation of patterns and schemes geared to promoting action (Sykes Wylie 2004).

Van der Kolk speculates that talking about the trauma may not be the source of healing. "Fundamentally words can't integrate the disorganized sensation and action patterns that form the core imprint of the trauma in the brain. Treatment needs to somehow incorporate the sensations and actions that have become stuck, so that people can regain a sense of familiarity and efficiency in their organism" (Van der Kolk 1994).

Dr. Van der Kolk reviews the neurobiological research on trauma. His findings conclude that trauma disrupts the stress hormone system, plays havoc with the entire nervous system, and keeps people from processing and integrating trauma memories into conscious mental frameworks (Sykes Wylie 2004, p.38). Van der Kolk believes that because these physiological processes are complex, the trauma stays stuck in the non-verbal, non-conscious subcortical regions of the brain. Such material often remains in the amygdala, thalamus, hypocampus or brain stem area where there is no access to the frontal lobes. The frontal lobes are most responsible for sorting things out, creating new insights and thinking or reasoning through material.

In his article "The body keeps the score" (1994), Van der Kolk elaborates on somatic body memory which relates well to Simone Weil's concept of how the muscles, nerves and flesh hold the imprint of terrifying events. Van der Kolk goes on to point out that understanding the physiological processes of the body, and particularly the physiological processes of the brain, has become critical to understanding how the body is central in the healing process.

In his book *The Instinct to Heal* (2004), David Servan-Schreiber documents the relationship between the emotional brain and the body. He describes how the digestive system and the heart have tens of thousands of neurons which act as mini brains. Without question the recording of emotional experiences is registered in our bodies. He goes on to illustrate in detail the function of the autonomic peripheral nervous system. The sympathetic branch which releases adrenaline and produces the fight or flight response works in conjunction with the parasympathetic branch which releases acetylcholine and promotes states of relaxation and calm which help in navigating unforeseen twists and turns in life. Both of these branches need to be equally strong. An overview describes the sympathetic branch as the gas pedal and the parasympathetic branch as the brake. Quite often in trauma situations there is a loss of the ability to utilize the brake. Further exploration reveals that maintaining the use of the parasympathetic branch is closely correlated with such activities as breathing, meditating, guided imagery, praying, imagining, art, dance, poetry and music.

In the book *Parenting from the Inside Out* (2003), by Siegel and Hartzell, there is more exploration of how the prefrontal cortex is instrumental in the resolution of trauma and loss. In their exploration of the right and left brain, they create a very specific analysis of how right mode and left mode processing are necessary to create wholeness and adaptability. Right mode processing includes non-linear, holistic, visual-spatial and autobiographical information. Left mode processing includes linear, logical, linguistic and more reasoning processes. When stories and autobiographical expressions are presented, a weaving between the two hemispheres is necessary in order to create a coherent and sensible narrative. The left brain helps to create the order and sequence of the actual events of the story, while the right brain supplies the feelings and sensations that make the story believable.

Re-telling the story or re-enacting the events is not only natural to children but is critical to good mental health and to their ability to learn. According to Jean Piaget "Children are informed by two related insights, that the child learns best by re-presenting her experience, and that all learning has an aesthetic component" (Elkind, Hetzel and Coe 1974). The concept that children learn by re-presenting their experience is congruent with the developmental understanding that children construct and re-create reality based on the interpersonal, social, cultural and experiential encounters that they have with the environment. Although Piaget does not speak directly to aesthetics, he elaborates on a concept of "equilibration" which is a concept that children will seek to create the most pleasing representation that is possible out of direct experience.

From a Piagetian view point, knowing the world is always an active process by which the child constructs reality out of his direct encounters with the world around him. This re-presenting process is not linear by nature but instead spiral as the construction process is ever expansive. At each stage of development and with each interruption of trauma, children reconstitute reality by actively manipulating and exploring. Motor and cognitive activities help to develop new schemas and concepts, re-creating and expanding on previous notions and perceptions.

When in fact children attempt to express their life experiences in aesthetically pleasing ways they are, in effect, striving for a new level of cognitive equilibration. Children are working both at an emotional and cognitive level to create more insight and integration between their re-presentations and their need to engage in the pleasurable enterprise of creating meaning. In essence whatever is true cognitively is also pleasing aesthetically. "Truth is beauty, is both an abstract aesthetic principle and a very practical rule of mental growth and development" (Elkind, Hetzel and Coe 1974, p.10).

Piaget has a strong belief in the importance of the child's point of view. His theories are highly respectful of the child's way of integrating and representing the world in which he lives. Piaget believes in the child's ability to make choices and judgments that lead to integration and perceptual change.

According to Stickgold (2002), Director of the Harvard Laboratory of Neurophysiology, EMDR (Eye Movement Desensitization Response) plays a primary role in reorganizing trauma memory in the brain. Research has begun to reveal that EMDR results in a reorientation of attention and produces a forced relaxation response. Such findings further illustrate the activity of the parasympathetic nervous system as a positive goal in trauma recovery.

Peter Levine, a body therapist who has created an approach to trauma treatment called Somatic Experiencing, seems to understand trauma as the "incomplete biological response to threat" (Levine 1997, p.40). According to Levine, "in humans when natural responses to danger are thwarted and people are helpless to prevent their own escape, or beating, or car accidents, or near death, the unfinished defensive actions become blocked as undischarged energy in their nervous systems" (Levine 1997, p.40). Levine believes that this interrupted action in humans still needs to be completed. Often he assists traumatized people in regaining their ability to move, to fight back, and to re-gain their ability to feel whole in their bodies as much as in their minds. Creating a safe place, Levine helps his clients to stay in touch with their bodies while re-experiencing the affects. Often this means allowing people to fight back safely in order to regain a sense of self-efficacy.

Action centered, Van der Kolk, Servan-Schreiber, Stickgold, Siegel and Hartzell, Piaget and Levine create a mind–body connection through their ability to stage moments of reflection whereby people can safely process what they cannot put into words. Both Homer and Weil reiterate these same tenents in their illustrations of how characters in *The Iliad* confront their fate with moments for insight, assistance and integration. Interestingly the expressive therapies of art, psychodrama, play, poetry, dance and movement were once called "the action therapies." Such expressive therapies grew from the need to give expression to non-verbal realities. Weil, Van der Kolk, and Levine allude to the fact that without safe reflection there is no ability to step out of dualistic realities. Such reflection often includes being open and vulnerable to larger truths. The non-dualistic, non-verbal languages of art, play, drama movement and the like form a spontaneous and immediate connection to body-centered, affectual awareness.

As has been mentioned, Weil makes a poignant analysis that the traumatized person finds that their days "hold no pastimes, no free spaces, no room in them for any impulse of their own" (Weil 1991, p.8). Rediscovering the possibility to become spontaneous, to release the interrupted action, to invoke the impulsive act, to create some freedom, to imagine healing, to open the creative space, is in fact to resolve some of the conflict that remains frozen or unexpressed. Establishing the safety and permission for such activity belongs to the creative. Understanding *The Iliad* and contemporary investigations of the human brain and body-centered therapies taxes our own ability to be free of judgment. In the complex maze of withheld reactions and responses, traumatic material challenges our ability to encompass the reality of the co-existence between compassion and violence, death and life, pain and joy, and the seemingly diverse nature of such entities. The more that we restrict and segregate ourselves and our affect from the freedom of expression and the freedom of reflection, the more we exile our selves from each other. Truly at the basis of such action-based theories is the basis of human discrimination. Honoring our most vulnerable citizens and upholding their human rights and human power is creating the safety of believing that we are not separate from their pain and suffering.

Simone Weil creates an image of herself as an activist who does not intellectually and emotionally separate herself from the people that she studies. Humble to their needs, she joins in their suffering and in their struggle to provide the most perfunctory acts. What is most critical is that she does not judge them, nor hold herself above their reality.

Conclusion

Historically cultures and organizations have found it most difficult to reflect on the larger more geometric process that naturally creates order. Such processes as the cycle of life and death, the struggle between good and evil, the reality of pain being a natural part of growth and development, the larger eco-systems and their impact on climatic change, the impact of national interests over global needs are easily neglected when focusing on more personal and self-serving concerns. Human creativity requires the individual to reckon with larger realities. The forces that are employed in *The Iliad* compel us to understand that only when we allow ourselves to reflect on our actions do we in fact open the door to humanity and the inclusion of ourselves as a necessary part of the larger picture of human suffering and pain. Re-presenting our life experiences calls forth the necessity of integrating highly diverse and complex notions of the world.

As long as people live with an inner feeling of angst and dread, with a sense of fear and avoidance feeling much more like a "thing" as Simone Weil so aptly describes the trauma that lives embedded in the body, they suffer more anguish than dying suddenly of a mortal wound and being forced into silence. There is no escape, only a constant need to never return to the event or the feelings associated with it. Whether hero or victim the truth is that there is no separation between the roles when we can see the larger picture. Entering a more expansive and geometric reality requires letting go of more conscious attachments and being open to complexity by allowing spontaneous re-presentations of affect as well as cognition.

It's not until memories move freely, spontaneously out of the amygdala to the prefrontal cortex that new insights, reflection and understanding occur. Stories both good and bad, both individual and collective need to be woven into the fabric of people's lives. Integration of such memories only occurs when new insights and understandings can be effectively attached to pre-existing knowledge, feelings and experiences. Rituals both individual and collective create an interplay between the familiar and the unknown.

When a culture, organization or family has a need to invalidate or suppress the expression of the meaning of pain, suffering, trauma, illness, human loss, grief and death as an ongoing reality in life, then it becomes unsafe and impossible for such realities to be seen, felt and integrated into the complex fabric and meaning of life itself.

Simone Weil, Bessel Van der Kolk, David Servan-Schreiber, Robert Stickgold, Jean Piaget, Peter Levine, and Homer would illustrate otherwise. Somehow we need to move into the non-dualistic reality whereby children and adults alike have the ability to hold the often dichotomous truth of how as human beings we need to make sense of the joy and pain in our lives with the help of relationships to discover more effective ways of communicating such realities. Contiguous with this notion is the ability to step back from the fight or flight response and discover new ways of re-focusing attention toward more open, less contrived notions about the complex world.

Human oppression as it may be expressed through poverty, human pain, grief, loss, death, and trauma represent the unspoken truth of a large percentage of society. Until such truths are not only honored but facilitated and integrated, human suffering continues to go unnoticed and yet pervades the lives and perceptions of its victims. Reflection or the ability to experience calmness while being confronted with chaos taps into human creativity. Action-centered responses engage the human body in utilizing sensory intelligences to explore and create balance. Praying, playing, dancing, singing, breathing, meditating, story telling, art and imagining provide the space for possibility, free choice and hope.

It is clear that through the tales of time come the wise and explicit messages about how life ultimately uncovers a journey into the unknown. The wisest amongst us engage in the journey uncovering new insights, awarenesses and possibilities of who we are and how we fit in the worlds in which we live. Letting go of knowing, each character, each adventure, challenge the person's ability to gain insights with the use of their bodies, muscles, senses, feelings, as well as their minds. Action leads the way as there is a constant need to work toward the goal of survival, insight and ultimate transformation.

The application of such insights can be seen in both clinical and community settings. The following tales are real; the truth will resonate with the reader at various levels. The authors take the theory base and look at the action components in many community settings. Although each application varies from site to site, the reader will gain awareness of the common variables that support and facilitate the creative autobiographic inner stories, dialogues and journeys that ultimately lead to change and transformation.

Teasing out the content both creative and expressive is a challenge. What cannot be put into words is often seen as non-existent. Cinderella, Hansel and Gretel, Chen, Sindbad, Achilles and Agamemnon suffer personal and significant trauma and loss. Utilizing the voice of imagination, literature illuminates what is often left in the shadow. More importantly the universal struggle for meaning, for love and acceptance, for deeper connections and possibilities becomes manifest in a world where complex realities can be supported and expressed. The world of symbolism opens the door for co-existence, for the acceptance of diversity and for the exploration of ultimate justice and peace. Co-existence of ambivalence, anger, injustice and confidence, love and peace become possible.

The human capacity to embrace ineffable realities is critical to our well-being. The writing attempts to capture how such realities are promoted in communities that hold acceptance, openness and loving support at the top of their list of values. Such communities dare to engage in the uncharted waters of chaos, anger and confusion. Amplified at every level of the literature is the message of how no one is separated from the force, that power which runs the universal concept of interconnection between nature and humanity. Trauma, pain and grief often move people toward positions of control.

The following community peer-supported programs look at what happens when there is enough love and support to let go of the control and express the underlying complexity of what leads to healing.

References

Acton, D. (2001) 'The "color blind" therapist.' *Art therapy: Journal of the American Art Therapy Association 18*, 2, 109–112.

Belanger, S.L. (1998) 'Knowing through art.' In W. Braud and R. Anderson (eds) *Transpersonal Research Methods for the Social Sciences*. Thousand Oaks, CA: Sage Publications.

Beiser, M., Turner, R.J. and Ganesan, S. (1989) 'Catastrophic stress and factors affecting its consequences among Southeast Asian refugees.' *Social Science and Medicine 28*, 3, 183–195.

Berry, J. W. (1998) 1Acculturation and health: theory and research.' In S. Kazarian and D. Evans (eds) *Cultural Clinical Psychology: Theory, Research and Practice*. New York: Oxford University Press.

Berry, J.W. and Bennett, J. (1989) 'Syllabic literacy and cognitive performance among the Cree.' *International Journal of Psychology 24*, 721–735.

Burvill, P.W. (1973) 'Immigration and mental disease.' *Australian and New Zealand Journal of Psychiatry 7*, 3, September, 155–162.

Cane, F. (1983) *The Artist in Each of Us.* Revised edition. Craftsbury Common, Vt: Art Therapy Publications.

Cervantes, R. C., Salgado de Snyder, V. N. and Padilla, A. M. (1989) 'Posttraumatic stress in immigrants from Central America and Mexico.' *Hospital & Community Psychiatry 40*, 615–619.

Douglas, B.C. (1993) 'Psychotherapy with troubled African American adolescent males: steretoypes, treatment amenability, and clinical issues.' In: The Annual Meeting of the American Psychological Association, August 1993, Toronto, Ontario, Canada.

Elkind, D, Hetzel, D. and Coe, J. (1974) 'Piaget and British Primary Education.' *Educational Psychologist 11*, 1, 1–10.

Fagan, N. (1998) 'Images and symbols.' In W. Braud and R. Anderson (eds) *Transpersonal Research Methods for the Social Science.* Thousand Oaks, CA: Sage Publications.

Farias, P.J. (1991) 'Emotional stress and its socio-political correlates in Salvadoran refugees: analysis of a clinical sample.' *Culture, Medicine and Psychiatry 15*, 167–192.

Goldberg, M. (2000) 'Conflicting principles in multicultural social work.' *Families in Society 81*, 12–21.

Greenfield, P.M. (1997) 'Culture as process: empirical methods for cultural psychology.' In J.W. Berry, Y.H. Poortinga and J. Pandey (eds) *Handbook of Cross-cultural Psychology.* Volume 1. Needman Heights, MA: Allyn & Bacon.

Hocoy, D. (1999) 'Working with Asian–American clients.' In J.V. Diller (ed) *Cultural Diversity: A Primer for Human Service Professionals.* Pacific Grove, CA: Brooks/Cole.

Homer, (1990) *The Iliad.* Translated from the Greek by R. Fagles. New York, NY: Viking.

Koff-Chapin, D. (1996) 'Touch drawing.' In W. Braud and R. Anderson *Transpersonal Research Methods for the Social Sciences.* Thousand Oaks, CA: Sage Publishers.

Levine, P. (1997) *Waking the Tiger; Healing Trauma: The Innate Capacity to Transform Overwhelming Experiences.* Berkeley, CA: North Atlantic Books.

Pendersen, P. (1988) *A Handbook for Developing Multicultural Awareness.* Alexandria, VA: American Association for Counseling and Development Press.

Piaget, J. (1967) *Six Psychological Studies.* New York: Random House.

Redfield, R., Linton, R. and Herskovits, M. (1936) 'Memorandum for the study of acculturation.' *American Anthropologist 38*, 149–150.

Samuda, R.J. (1990) *New Approaches to Assessment and Placement of Minority Students.* Toronto: MGS.

Samuda, R.J. and Wolfgang, A. (eds) (1985) *Intercultural Counseling and Assessment: Global Perspective.* Lewiston, NY: C.J. Hogrefe.

Servan-Schreiber, D. (2004) *The Instinct to Heal.* Emmaus, PA: Rodale.

Siegel, D.J. and Hartzell, M. (2003) *Parenting from the Inside Out.* New York, NY: Penguin Group.

Stickgold, R. (2002) 'A putative neurobiological mechanism.' *Journal of Clinical Psychology 58*, 61–75.

Sykes Wylie, M. (2004) 'The limits of talk.' *Psychotherapy Networker.* January/February, 30–36, 38–41, 67.

Van der Kolk, B.A. (1994) 'The body keeps the score: memory and the emerging psychobiology of post traumatic stress.' *Harvard Review of Psychiatry 1*, 253–265.

Van der Kolk, B.A., McFalene, A.C. and Weisaeth, L. (1996) *Traumatic Stress.* New York: Guilford Press.

Weil, S. (1991) *Iliad or the Poem of Force.* Twelfth edition Wallingford, PA: Pendle Hill Publications.

CHAPTER 2

The Center for Grieving Children

Introduction

The purpose of this chapter is to present a case study of using the arts and creative approaches with children from a range of different cultures. This model combines a peer support theory coupled with the introduction of specific arts materials and creative processes centered on the emerging themes from a multicultural group of children. The multicultural group is a part of programs offered by the Center For Grieving Children in collaboration with the Portland Maine Public Schools. Portland Maine is an urban city of approximately 64,000 people. It still has a more rural identity based on its close ties and connections to a highly rural state. Within the city itself are combinations of well-developed cultural and environmental resources. Having a sea port identity Portland combines urban living with numerous recreational opportunities.

Immigrant families often seek Portland as a desirable home site from other resettlement communities in the United States as well as a primary destination from their countries of origin. Catholic Charities is one of the host organizations helping families settle in the Portland area. Families frequently choose the Portland community because it has a safe, friendly, small and supportive community base. Especially important are the health, educational and social services for children and families.

With over nine years of operation, the Multicultural Program at the Center For Grieving Children has reached out to over five hundred children. Collaboration has included the Portland Public Schools, the University of Southern Maine, University of New England, Lesley University and a host of community organizations including the African Museum, Portland Museum of Art, Parks and Recreation, the Libra Foundation (a private, philanthropic organisation established by the late Elizabeth Noyce), United Way (a non-profit organization that raises money for community organizations), the Maine College of Art and Peoples Regional Opportunity Program (PROP; a community action agency committed to identifying and addressing social, economic, education and health needs). Such collaborations have offered direct services and enrichment for the children as well as structured support for the program.

The Multicultural Program provides a group process that is facilitated by trained volunteers as well as supervised interns. Intrinsic to this program is the opportunity for children to express verbally and non-verbally the under-lying losses and traumas associated with a multitude of life-changing events. Most children have had no control over the loss of language, culture, homeland, native foods, religious practices, holidays and the actual deaths of family members.

Paying attention to the needs of multicultural children in transition, this program follows the lead of children by providing physical, creative and contextual languages that encourage free expression and communication. Readers will begin to find connections between highly individual vignettes and previous connections made between the literature and mythic structures.

Traditionally group programs focus on social, behavioral, cognitive, affective aspects of the self. Because of the multicultural implications the focus shifts into the cultural, political and spiritual notions of self and community. What becomes more apparent are the indigenous helping methods and practices which exist within these communities and families.

The Center for Grieving Children

The Center for Grieving Children is a non-profit organization committed to offering a safe environment for children, teens, and adults to express and heal grief through peer support groups and outreach programs. The Center serves children, teens, families, schools, and communities that are coping with the life-threatening illness of a family member or friend, or grieving over the death of a loved one. Its programs are well established in the Portland, Maine community and serve as a resource for developing other centers throughout the state of Maine. The program is based on collaboration through peer support. All volunteers are aware of the Center's five guiding principles:

- Grieving is a natural response to change, loss, and the death of a loved one.

- Grief is individual and has its own time and duration.

- Within each individual, child or adult, is the natural ability to heal oneself.

- Caring and acceptance assist in the healing process.

- We honor the diverse cultural and spiritual beliefs of all who come to the Center.

Background of the Multicultural Program

One of the Center's operating programs is the Multicultural Program. This program was established in 1997, as a result of the death of a Cambodian child. At that time the Center did outreach to the community and established a group built on its operating principles along with the inclusion of the arts. This outreach peer support group became the pilot study and introduction to the deeper needs of children in the multicultural community.

Each group was facilitated by at least two volunteers. Every volunteer at the Center has gone through a peer support training, whereby they have not only understood the Center's guiding principles but have also explored their own grief and loss. Facilitators in the Multicultural Program have additional training focused on both research and actual experience in facilitating multicultural groups. Groups at the Center average between four and six participants. Each group is clustered with peers of similar ages and similar developmental stages. Group facilitators are trained to listen and facilitate communication between peers. A Tornado Room becomes an integrated part of the program. This room has two additional facilitators who help individuals or pairs of children express body-centered affect in a safe, padded, and well-equipped facility. Children can be physically active using boxing gloves with a punch bag or quiet activities involving stacking foam blocks and creating safe hiding places. Arts materials and games become additional support mediums within the group process.

Trusting that children have their own mode of communication concerning the expression of grief and loss, the groups are not highly structured. Instead rituals such as opening check-in, sharing past and present stories, and occasional group-driven events interface with the open agenda of supporting children's natural abilities to name and explore their grief. Each facilitator also receives peer support by having one hour before groups to check in, letting go of events in their own lives that may interfere with being present to the children. This ritual also affords for group peer connections, support and intimacy. In addition a debriefing hour occurs after each group in order to help facilitators identify their personal responses to the process and to gain support and insight.

The Multicultural Program is in session during the regular school year. Although the members of the groups are also peers in their academic program, the Center represents a very different level of relating. Opening circles engage children in games and activities along with eating rituals that help make the transition from school to the Center. Smaller individual peer groups build trust and support individual and group expression. The themes and ritual activities around loss and grief unfold as children find the group safe and supportive. Building safety and trust, facilitators convey a belief in children's innate resilience and look for strengths and assets as opposed to problems and deficits. Children are supported in expressing their own values and developing responsibility within their peer groups. Rituals and practices within the groups afford many opportunities for making decisions, for giving voice and being heard, and for contributing one's talents, abilities, and creativity within the group. Consultants who have a variety of mental health backgrounds such as clinical counseling, licensed clinical social workers, faculty from schools of social work, professionals from the University of Southern Maine and other mental health providers give direct programmatic support to the Multicutural Program and its facilitators and other staff. Staff co-ordinators direct the program and facilitate communication between the program, facilitators, the Portland Public Schools and other community organizations. Both consultants and staff co-ordinators work closely to support the ongoing mental health needs of both the participants and the facilitators.

A typical program day opens with an opening ritual. After the children leave their bus and come to the large group room, activities are directed toward engaging the children's energy through specific games and activities that offer structure and support for entry into the program. Next children are directly connected to each other through a large circle activity usually centered around sharing names and familiar stories and information. Food is typically shared in the large group and then children move into smaller rooms where they join two facilitators who develop a creative process and a peer supported relationship where not more than four children begin to creatively express and socially explore some of the losses associated with their movement from other world communities and their omnipresent acculturation process. Children develop safety and trust as they identify many of the hardships such as being cultural brokers for their parents as well as language translators and the multifaceted problems of racism and discrimination within the dominant culture. During the time spent in individual groups children have the opportunity to visit the Tornado Room. Closing rituals move back to the larger room where again the entire community becomes the focus and the purpose.

In the course of over nine years of operation the Multicultural Program has changed. What we have learned from children has been instrumental in such changes as lowering the group size to four members, designing opening games and rituals that were highly active, participating in community-based multicultural events and community-based dominant culture events, recognizing the importance and magnitude of building trust and of forming better communications and collaborations with the Portland Public Schools and with the children's parent community.

Community multicultural history

Children from South East Asia, Africa, Russia and China make up the social and ethnic fabric of Portland, Maine, the largest city in the state. Catholic Charities of Maine has a strong refugee resettlement program, which has placed over 5000 refugees in the Portland community in the past 20 years. Maine's refugee resettlement program is somewhat unusual in that most of the resettlement has occurred in one city, rather than being scattered throughout the state. With a population of approximately 64,000, Portland is challenged to integrate this large and ethnically diverse population. Catholic Charities of Maine does not work with refugees from only one nation or region of the world, but rather accepts refugees from a variety of nations. No one immigrant group dominates. A large percentage of immigrants who at first settle elsewhere in the United States often choose Maine as a second or third home because of its "peaceful, quiet" reputation. Many of the families come to Portland from other cities because they hear that Portland offers a good education and a safe upbringing for their children.

As a result, Portland has the most diverse elementary schools in the state. Forty per cent of students come from households where English is not the primary language. Over 42 different languages are spoken, among them Serbo-Croatian, Khmer, Vietnamese, Somali, Spanish, Arabic, Russian, and the African language of Acholi.

Schools have had to address the complex challenges of cognitive, social, and language integration. The police department has had to deal with issues unfamiliar to them, such as tribal rivalries and cultural beliefs that are divergent from western values and laws. Creative and collaborative efforts have been made by the educational, social welfare and law enforcement communities to join these diverse communities. Peer leadership programs and civilian co-ordinators who come from the Asian, Chinese, African, and Russian communities collaborate with the police department, schools, the Center and the children and families themselves.

As a result of community collaborations, many of the immigrants have formed organizations that benefit refugee camps and help their relatives and friends to flee starvation and sickness. The Action for Self Reliance Association (ASERELA), for example, is a group of more than 100 Sudanese immigrants who have escaped civil wars. This organization has sponsored a fundraiser for the Kiryandogo Refugee Camp in Uganda. Such fundraisers are community collaborations that both educate and facilitate awareness and integration.

History of the Multicultural Program

Assisting a multiethnic group of children and adolescents who have experienced violent and traumatic events in their life is a daunting task. A primary focus was to promote creative personal expression within a supportive peer community. Due to forced migration, multigenerational tragedy, cultural changes, war or armed conflict, death of family members or community members, developmental needs, and language differences, working with complex grief and trauma becomes a difficult task.

In 1997, the Cambodian community in Portland was deeply shaken by the murder of a 12-year-old Cambodian boy. The death brought up many issues of loss in Portland's Cambodian community. Working with PROP, the Center for Grieving Children acted very quickly in creating a grief and loss program for children who were greatly impacted by this event. The Center offered a safe place where these children were allowed to express their feelings, particularly the safe and healthy expression of anger. The facilitators soon learned that the children who were grieving were also in touch with some of their own personal and cultural losses that had occurred as a result of their own loss of family members and loss of geographic, ethnic, familial, cultural and language traditions.

Over the next year the Center, in collaboration with PROP, obtained funding to provide two six-week sessions to 12 youths impacted by loss. Themes of violence and loss both associated with the past, and with the multiple complex histories of the participants, began to emerge. Children and adolescents needed to have a safe place to process their grief. Their grief encompassed current traumatic experiences, as well as those from previous generations. Having a chance to access, boldly express, creatively produce and name their feelings and memories, not only released the anger and grief but also created the opportunity to learn non-violent ways of coping. Art and puppetry were an important action medium for this group process. Puppetry became an important action event that both engaged the playful instincts of each child and ultimately formed a group process for play and communication. During one puppet play a dragon emerged as an all-powerful character who was merciless toward all other animals. One by one other puppet animals: the rabbit, the cow, the bear, the wolf, etc., all tried to stop the angry onslaught of the dragon's aggressive attacks. The dragon was impossible to stop, and each character was jumped on physically or verbally dismissed and frightened away. Within the group of participants several girls started to cry and talked about how abused and mistreated they had felt as the victims of physical fights, personal conflicts and violence. References to violence were inclusive of events from their countries of origin as well as events of racism and oppression within their present communities. Often families face opposing refugee groups from their own country who have resettled in Portland, Maine.

Deepening the experience, children were then asked to create a personal puppet that represented power in the natural or imaginative world. The tiger, a person in blue coveralls, a rabbit, a bumblebee, a fighter, an owl and various imaginative puppets emerged as children drew and decorated their power symbols. Triads were formed whereby children had the opportunity to state a personal need and to have the other two puppets respond. Children expressed their fears about gang games on the street, shared about their long and difficult journey of coming to Portland, Maine, confided about their needs for peer support and shared what it was like to feel alone or rejected in their school peer groups because of their cultural differences. Themes of care, friendship, concern and human support emerged as children felt safe enough to step back from their pain, share some of their anger and ask for peer support and help.

Activities in the Tornado Room included aggressive and fun play, hitting a large punching bag, using loud voices, playing with foam noodles, pillows and other padded equipment. Children soon began to express their fears about strangers breaking into their homes in Somalia and the Sudan. Some children talked about fighting on the streets of their village. Others went on to describe the unpredictable destruction of their homes and the deaths of family members.

In another group process children completed Mandala drawings. "Mandala" is Sanskrit for circle. Often mandalas are the central design in hand-woven prayer rugs. Mandala drawings utilize a circle format rather than a rectangular space. As a result the drawing is not limited to drawing norms. Children were asked to draw symbols from the journey representing transitions from their homeland to the United States. Often their drawings had rich and detailed images of the homes and landscapes that they came from. Conversations emerged about the sadness and loss of personal belongings, family pets, relatives, familiar rituals and routines pertaining to their homelands. Of particular significance were the re-occurring images of jet planes. Many children expressed spontaneously their first encounters with western foods, language and media. Most of the children disliked the foods, signage, language, smells and sounds. Such new sensory encounters seemed foreign and overwhelming.

Within the Center's ritual activities, stones are frequently used for closing and recognition symbols. The qualities of such stones are verbalized as support and recognition. For example, pink quartz represents love and nurturance. The children became enthralled with this ritual and decided to create their own power stones. Selecting stones from a bowl, group members personally decorated their stones with power symbols. Children used acrylic paints to complete their task. It is of particular interest that most children utilized symbols that were connected to their own culture of origin. These symbols most frequently related to nature. The sun, the moon, stars, serpents, lions, trees, the sea and other natural symbols dominated their imagery. Some of the children created power images from the western culture relating to characters from Pokemon and Dragonballzi, which are western video games.

Conclusion

The Center for Grieving Children in Portland, Maine offers a safe place for children from South East Asia, Africa, Russia and China to express some of their underlying conflicts related to their forced migration, multigenerational tragedy, cultural changes, war or armed conflict, death, losses and language differences. What is even more profound is that most children and their families have moved to the United States for safety and protection and yet the dominant culture presents additional stresses and conflict related not only to acculturation but also to issues of racism, economic survival and family conflict. Quite often the children are the language interpreters for their own parents. While the parents protect the rituals of their culture of origin, the children are quickly forced into an accelerated acculturation process.

The Center for Grieving Children has a peer support structure that facilitates the natural social, creative and physical action necessary in promoting expression and communication within the safety and trust of a community.

Once safety and trust is established children can actually be leaders in their own healing and acculturation. Children's spontaneous and creative actions and expressions open the door to gaining insight and awareness of the often complex path toward resolving underlying trauma and grief.

CHAPTER 3

Children, Our Greatest Teachers

Introduction

Seldom do we think of children as teachers. Certainly children do not have the life experiences or knowledge of their seniors. However, children are much more in tune with their sensory intelligence, which is not easily accessible or readily available for adults. When considering the cultures of family traditions, political practices, pedagogy, theology, social standards, and mythological roots, they are taught through cognition and practiced non-verbally. Non-verbal realitiesc are more observable and more impactful for children. In fact children navigate in non-verbal realities with more ease and flexibility. The rituals, standards and practices of everyday life, along with the deeper cultural values, are being absorbed and assimilated by children. When war, trauma, violence, and loss interrupt the fabric of meaningful life, children are gravely impacted and instrumentally resourceful. Resilience in persevering is only usurped by the ability to remain open and flexible to understand the importance of the child's ability to engage in pleasurable activity in spite of underlying tragedy. Action-centered children are natural in their capacity to both heal and transform. This process can only take place when there is adult leadership and support to build the trust and relationship necessary for children to engage freely with their own resources.

The impact of war on children and adolescents

The growing literature suggests that children's psychological reactions may differ from those of adults in that the responses may be more transient and less severe. Studies of Israeli and Palestinian children and children from

Northern Ireland indicated a notable decrease in stress reaction with lapse of time (Klingman 1992; Lyons 1971; Punamaki and Suleiman 1990). Residual stress reactions were detected, particularly among children with high immediate stress and with high degrees of stress exposure (Solomon 1995). When extremely violent war events directly touch a child's nuclear family, the psychological effects may become serious. A study of the long-term impact 20 years after the terrorist attack involving the seizure of Israeli high school students as hostages (Desivilya, Gal and Ayalon 1996) revealed that although most survivors exhibited relatively high levels of adaptation, the traumatic experience at adolescence had a long-lasting effect on the survivor's adult life. This effect has been noted in interpersonal and intrapersonal domains, as well as in their emotional response in emergency situations, such as the Gulf War of 1991.

Several studies have found that children with high exposure to war reported more significant adverse emotional, cognitive, and physiological symptoms than those residing in areas less exposed to war events and may sustain more long-term damage (Klingman 1992; Rosenthal and Levy-Shiff 1993; Schwartzwald *et al.* 1993).

Somatic and health indicators are affected by trauma. Studies with Kuwaiti children following the Gulf Wars showed a link between proximity to war violence and increased self-reported somatic symptoms and complaints.

Growing up in a war-affected community may promote aggressive behavior in children, at least in some cultural contexts (Garbarino, Kostelny and Dubrow 1991; McCloskey and Southwick 1996). Children's experience of war-related trauma has been linked to an increase in aggressiveness, some increase in juvenile delinquency (Muldoon and Cairns 1999), and problems with impulse control (Nader and Fairbanks 1994). A broad range of daily activities, such as reckless and inconsiderate driving and externalization of rage towards authority figures, is seen in the war-torn Israeli society (Klingman, Sagi and Ravi 1993).

Adolescents are less dependent than young children on their parents and adult mentors and tend to respond more to the world beyond their families. Developmental psychologists are increasingly recognizing that late adolescence is a time when socio-political influences on identity are particularly powerful. A political ideology and commitment may help buffer the experience of war by allowing adolescents to interpret their experiences as "necessary evil" that must be endured if ideological objectives are to be achieved (Garbarino and Kostelny 1993; Muldoon and Cairns 1999).

Coping and adaptation

The impact of war stress on children depends considerably on both personal coping capacity and environmental support. Young children's resilience depends considerably on their parents' stress absorption and their parents' and significant others' support, whereas individual dispositions and interpretations of their situational (and environmental) control play a greater part for older children and adolescents. For adolescents, war often brings out a strength and energy unlike anything seen at other times.

Staying active, as through involvement in helpful behaviors (Hobfoll *et al.* 1991), can help children gain a sense of mastery and control over their lives despite the ordeal and keep their minds off the dangers of the war. Children were encouraged to become engaged in artwork and art exhibition. The activities enabled them to ventilate feelings and keep them occupied, active, and creative (Shilo-Cohen 1993).

Children must gain positive expectation. The lack of experience with the adversities of war and the war being a protracted crisis, may lead children to exaggerate their problems and prevent them from seeing "light at the end of the tunnel" (Hobfoll *et al.* 1991). Children therefore should be helped to not catastrophize and are encouraged to gain perspective and view situational setbacks and psychological lapses as part of a "normal" process of war.

The long-term prognosis of children exposed to war hinges, in large measure, on the ability of the adult community to be psychologically available to children, to reassure and protect them, and to clarify and interpret the experience (Garbarino and Kostelny 1993). Although experiencing helplessness and exposure to violence are likely to cause regression in a youngster's development (e.g. delays in attaining independence, identity formation, establishing trust and intimacy), such patterns can be minimized by the availability of a highly cohesive support system (Caplan 1964; Garmezy 1985; Klingman 2001; Ziv and Israeli 1973). For those experiencing long-term separation from both parents, the mobilization of community resources is vital.

Children who grow up during war need to "make sense" of their experiences; thus, telling them about the war is important. Once children know or feel that a danger exists, they need to have a concrete picture of how adults around them will deal with the dangers. School-aged children may demand to know exactly what lies ahead of them and what they will be expected to do; talking about and imaging events in a gradual, controlled way before they happen can forestall the fears. The events they see portrayed in the media should be discussed and explained while maintaining as calm, confident, and reassuring an attitude as possible under the circumstances. The experience of hearing war-related topics spoken of by significant others in a calm and reasonable manner helps relieve children from hidden worries and is reassuring. Overwhelmed by the war, adults must guard against vivid descriptions of their own fears when in the presence of young children. Monitoring of children's television viewing is important, and it is best for adults to watch with them.

Some children distance themselves, whereas others show remarkable willingness to talk about their deeply troubling war experiences and welcome the opportunity to do so (Berman 1999). Children should be helped to understand at least some of the factors that led to the war and the types of weapons that are involved. They should be instructed about situation-specific precautions, safety measures, and family emergency plans, but they should also be allowed to communicate their concerns and ventilate their worries in a supportive and positive context.

The continuity principle

Consistent with the major findings from disaster and trauma research, Omer and Alon (1994) suggested and developed the continuity principle to provide concrete applicable guidelines for decision making and treatment under severe conditions. It stipulates that throughout all stages of the war cycle, intervention should be aimed at preserving and restoring continuity that has been disrupted as a result of war. The more an intervention is built on the child's existing individual, familial, organizational, and communal (e.g. schools, neighborhood support services) strengths and resources, the more effective it will be in counteracting the disruptive effects of war.

Every available material, every person, and every event can become "therapeutic" if used to help a child advance in the direction of bridging some breach in continuity (Alon and Levine Bar-Yoseph 1994). Intervention efforts should be swift and as simple as possible, and they should have a clear goal of normalization of stress reactions.

Restoring personal (historical) continuity includes seeing the child's basic needs orienting the child to what led to the war and the plans for him or her for the near future encouraging the child to talk about the experience until as clear and full a picture as possible is obtained; ascribing meaning to and re-framing the situation; regarding the child's emotional responses as being a normal transitory process of adaptation and clearly presenting positive expectations. The mental anguish is gradually processed and integrated into the child's perceived world.

Restoring interpersonal continuity involves establishing or enhancing interpersonal support with significant others. Restoration of social bonds includes the enhancement of solidarity of the group; such bonds provide the strongest protection against despair and an antidote to war experience. Restoring functional continuity on the personal level involves encouraging even minimal and simple situation-specific activities that can be executed at a given time by the child.

Restoring organizational continuity means taking action to rebuild the child's sense of order and continuity in the familiar neighborhood. In this context school is of extreme importance. Through the school system, mental health teams can reach out to children and families to advise them on proper situation-specific versus negative reactions of children and on desirable ways of coping they can encourage and reinforce.

Therapeutic interventions

Interventions frequently oscillate between a focus on problems in daily living and exploration of traumatic war experiences. Creating a safe environment and strengthening the child's feelings of safety and trust must take priority. The most widely used and, apparently, effective approaches are short-term, trauma-focused interventions that provide reassurance and support while gradually, often indirectly, exploring the war experiences. Subsequently, the child is helped to gradually uncover the traumatic war experiences to make sense of the overwhelming experiences and to identify and express the underlying affect necessary for the healing to take place. The interventions often combine selected elements of both dynamic and cognitive-behavioral therapies. The intervention must be age-appropriate and conducted at the child's own pace.

Assessment considerations

Research on children's responses to war and on therapeutic intervention with children in war has been much sparser on the whole than the study of adults. This difference is attributed to the methodological, ethical, and practical problems entailed in studying children (Jensen 1996; Klingman 1992, 2001; Klingman *et al.* 1993). It is also difficult to draw definitive empirical conclusions from some of the research, given the inevitable absence of control groups in war time. The responses of young children to war have been the least studied as a result of the difficulties inherent in assessing children too young to fill in questionnaires or even speak.

Berman (1999) assessed refugee children of war using an audiotape interviewing approach that, unlike a traditional interview format, followed a theoretical and methodological perspective that encouraged children to "name their reality," critically reflect on that reality, and consider strategies for changing that reality if desired.

Keeping in mind the methodological constraints embedded in those procedures, they nevertheless further our understanding of young children's affective reactions and coping in war circumstances. Moreover, the procedures appear to engage children's interest, ensure a high level of motivation, and minimize evaluative anxiety. In addition, they have therapeutic value in themselves because they serve as an outlet for ventilation of children's fears and anxieties.

Strategies for working with children who have experienced war

Through understanding children's responses to war, it becomes possible to determine the most effective ways of helping them cope. Young children are influenced most heavily by the attitudes and actual responses of their caregivers. Therefore it is important for children not to be separated from their natural support system and for preventative intervention efforts to be aimed at providing caregivers with the resourcefulness to help children adapt to the altered circumstances that war presents. For older children and adolescents, both parents and educators play a vital role in buffering the experiences of war and determining children's responses to the adversities of war; educators have particular opportunities to integrate preventative measures in the context of wide-ranging curricula.

Within the Multicultural Program, adult volunteers as well as the peer group offer effective ways in which children can cope with their responses to wars, and to their multiple losses. Creating a climate of safety and building interpersonal trust the Center for Grieving Children's program sets the stage for safe play, socialization and creative process. Within that context there exists enough safety whereby children begin to share stories related to their acculturation experience as well as significant and often traumatic stories of the past. Personal stories are supported and this safe environment promotes the affective expression of anger through art and in the Tornado Room. Just behind the fury and chaos lie the deeper feelings of loss and grief. Adult facilitators become aware of the complexity associated with the affective as well as cultural barriers to expression. Spontaneity in behavior as well as creative expression becomes key to the process of change. Mentors are challenged to take on unorthodox and creative approaches towards both engaging and determining resolution to such diverse feeling realities.

Maps in each of the rooms are used as a quick way to trace the moves, changes and transitions. One Sudanese boy refers to the map and explains how he and his family had to move from the Sudan to Egypt in order to get a flight to America. He says that only the wealthy can go directly, that his family and thousands of others wait, wait and wait until they can make the trip. His father made the trip before the rest of the family and ended up in Portland, Maine. But he and his brother and mother ended up a year later in Dallas, Texas and later were able to move to Portland to be together as a family. Other children in the group verify that they too had difficult journeys to America. Stories come up in the group about what it was like being in Egypt.

Art activities sometimes make a similar transition from the present moment into the past, often painful losses and traumas. A Cambodian adolescent girl drops red paint onto a clay shape that she has created. As the red, black and white drops of paint, like drops of blood, create her dotted object, she reflects on the family members who were killed in the Killing Fields. Tears form in her eyes and in her peers' and facilitators' as she sadly talks about the family members that she will never see again. Structures both in the human relationships and in the relationship with materials and images foster the many ways that children name their reality, release the affect and discover new insights and awarenesses about the content.

Epiphany-like, the images rest in the mind like the words of a sonnet, poem or the rhythm of Beethoven's "Moonlight" Piano Sonata, or Cinderella's plight and recovery, the image of Van Gogh's "Starry Night," all haunting and familiar at the same time. The images from the Multicultural Program of the Killing Fields, the dragon's destruction, the stories, and the endless essay of imagery that children create as a symbol, talisman-like, unfold as a gateway to grounding their experiences, thereby counteracting the disruptive effects of war.

Wisdom through the ages, stories, images, folk tales, fairy tales, poems, music, icons, and writings all capture creative moments when the doorway opens to deeper, more unconscious truths that connect humanity to each other and to the natural world. Connecting rather than fragmenting imagination strengthens the child's ability to play and normalize otherwise conflictual material.

Lasting longer than cultures or civilizations and their history are the mythic artifacts made permanent through the story and image. Perceptual by nature, the human mind holds the precious memories, past, present and future, negative and positive, oppressive and hopeful, self-centered and generative, nurturing and truthful, as stepping stones to reality. Collective truth emerges when the mythic structures hold truth that is shared across humanity, that holds inherent insights about the natural world and that is inclusive and hopeful about the meaning of existence.

Jewel-like are the stories, images and actions that emerge from children spontaneously. Putting pleasure over principle, the young child leads by investigating the truth without consciously defined rules. Familial, religious, cultural and pedagogical structures are certainly important to development and progress but are at times counter-productive to taking risks with learning and discovering the inner resources to navigate through life's struggles and celebrations.

Spontaneous movement, imagery and verbalization are a direct source to the underlying, often unconscious feelings that are stored within our bodies. Creative process allows for dualistic realities of negative and positive, conscious and unconscious, etc. to co-exist. Non-discriminatory by nature, play, free association, spontaneous writing, spontaneous imagery, free drama and the like allow such dualistic notions of life to emerge and be expressed.

Adventurous by nature, children will explore such opposite realities with openness and enthusiasm if the facilitator is open themselves. Easily led and instructed by adults, children will follow or read unconscious direction provided by adults. Reflected in the teaching stories called parables, or in the creation stories of mythology, or in the richly symbolic fairy tales and folklore, lies the wisdom of the ages. Within these stories and within our own personal stories are the powerful images that can uncover the intrinsic ability that people have to heal their own pain.

The attitude and responses of the facilitators in the Multicultural Program help form the trust and well-being of the children. For many of the children, establishing positive connections and relationships with the facilitators and with their peers is a first step in the healing process. Such support signals a return to normality and an inclusion that sponsors trust and communication as a way through some of the conflict and turmoil associated with change, loss, trauma and acculturation.

Invitations into the patterns, rituals and holidays of the dominant culture, balanced by observations of the patterns, rituals and holidays of the multiple cultures is an avenue of support, recognition and normalization. Rich with cultural heritage in dealing with change, eastern cultures and indigenous and Third World cultures are well recognized for their abilities to understand healing as revealed in the roles of the medicine man, chiefs, shamans, teachers and seers as the "change masters" (Young 1996). Children from world cultures reflect many of these traditions and have much to teach western civilization about being present, paying attention to what has meaning for the heart, to tell the truth and to not judge the process or be attached to outcomes.

Western culture, other than through indigenous Native Americans, is more separated from healing and creation myth structures. Children remind us that personal and cultural myths are the fertile ground of where meaning for life, existence and future is forged. They still believe that they can turn to nature, imagination, ritual, art, stories, creativity and the like to re-discover what in fact gives their personal and social lives meaning. Such activities are natural, human mechanisms that not only provide the continuity in everyday life but also serve to integrate fragmentation, trauma, leading to transformation.

Conclusion

Children still dare to question what has meaning. From the tenets of world-wide myths to the order of the natural world and the complex social, political fabric of life, children remain open, questioning and flexible when they receive the love, trust and support from their adult mentors to do so. Being able to offer normalized approaches to safely holding such content and at the same time being open to deeper explorations challenges the logical mindset.

Modeling such openness and flexibility is not the norm of adult behavior. Not knowing is both a source of adult discomfort and angst. Because children are still in formational stages of both their development and cognition, they are less directed by the acculturated norms, rules and standards of the adult world.

Whatever human ways that children choose to withdraw from pain or not repeat what traumas have happened to them, the less apt they are to be spontaneous. Children will often curtail their play and creativity by presenting controlling behaviors. In fact, the defenses that they have learned by displacing, denying or avoiding the triggers of their own loss are the inhibitors to their own natural healing. Vulnerable feelings cannot safely be expressed until there exists trust and support to do so.

Empowered by the trust, safety and support from adult mentors and peers, children display openly the resilience and highly skilled abilities to self-heal. In settings where such factors are in place children lead with their creative instincts. Flexibility and openness to express inner pathways to knowing represent the highly evolved ways in which children become our greatest teachers. Adults' ability to trust not knowing and to trust the leadership of the child's healing instincts challenge conscious notions of how the social, cultural, informational and political worlds operate.

References

Alon, N. and Levine Bar-Yoseph, T. (1994) 'An approach to the treatment of post traumatic stress disorder (PTSD).' In P. Clarkson and M. Pokorny (eds) *The Handbook of Psychotherapy*. New York: Routledge.

Berman, H. (1999) 'Stories of growing up amid violence by refugee children of war and children of battered women living in Canada.' *Image: Journal of Nursing Scholarship 31*, 57–63.

Caplan, G. (1964) *Principles of Preventive Psychiatry*. New York: Basic Books.

Desivilya, H.S., Gal, R. and Ayalon, O. (1996) 'Long-term effects of trauma in adolescence: comparison between survivors of a terrorist attack and control counterparts.' *Anxiety, Stress, and Coping 9*, 135–150.

Garbarino, J. and Kostelny, K. (1993) 'Childrens response to war.' In L.A. Leavitt and N.A. Fox (eds) *The Psychological Effects of War and Violence on Children*. Hillsdale, NJ: Erlbaum Associates.

Garbarino, J., Kostelny, K. and Dubrow, N. (1991) *No Place to be a Child: Growing Up in a War Zone*. New York: Lexington Books.

Garmezy, N. (1985) 'Stress-resistant children: the search for protective factors.' In J.E. Stevenson (ed) *Recent Research in Developmental Psychopathology*. Oxford: Pergamon Press.

Hobfoll, S.E., Spielberger, C.D., Breznitz, S., Figley, C., Folkman, S., Lepper-Green, B., Meichenbaum, D., Milgram, N.A., Sandler, I., Sarason, I. and van der Kolk, B. (1991) 'War-related stress: addressing the stress of war and other traumatic events.' *American Psychologist 46*, 8 August, 848–856.

Jensen, P.S. (1996) 'Practical approaches to research with children in violent settings.' In R.J. Apfel and B. Simon (eds) *Minefields in their Hearts: The Mental Health of Children in War and Communal Violence.* New Haven, CT: Yale University Press.

Klingman, A. (1992) 'Stress reactions of Israeli youth during the gulf war: a quantitative study.' *Personal and Guidance Journal 57,* 22–26.

Klingman, A. (2001) 'Stress responses and adaptation of Israeli school-aged children evacuated from homes during massive missile attacks.' *Anxiety, Stress and Coping 14,* 2 May, 149–173.

Klingman, A. Sagi, A. and Ravi, A. (1993) 'The effects of war on Israeli children.' In L.A. Leavitt and N.A. Fox (eds) *The Psychological Effects of War and Violence on Children.* Hillsdale, NJ: Erlbaum Associates.

Lyons, H.A. (1971) 'Psychiatric sequels of the Belfast riots.' *Psychiatry 118,* 265–273.

McCloskey, L.A. and Southwick, K. (1996) 'Psychological problems in refugee children exposed to war.' *Pediatrics 97,* 394–397.

Muldoon, O. and Cairns, E. (1999) 'Children, young people, and war: learning to cope.' In E. Frydenberg (ed) *Learning to Cope: Developing as a Person in Complex Societies.* Oxford: Oxford University Press.

Nader, K. and Fairbanks, L.A. (1994) 'The suppression of re-experiencing: impulse control and somatic symptoms in children following traumatic exposure.' *Anxiety, Stress and Coping 7,* 229–239.

Omer, H. and Alon, N. (1994) 'The continuity principle: a unified approach to disaster and trauma.' *American Journal of Community Psychology 22,* 2, 273–287.

Punamaki, R.L. and Suleiman, R. (1990) 'Predictors and effectiveness of coping with political violence among Palestinan children.' *British Journal of Social Psychology 29,* 67–77.

Rosenthal, M. and Levy-Shiff, R. (1993) 'Threat of missile attacks in the Gulf War: mothers' perceptions of young children's reactions.' *American Journal of Orthopsychiatry 63,* 241–254.

Schwartzwald, J., Weisenberg, M., Waysman, M., Solomon, Z. and Klingman, A. (1993) 'Stress reaction of school-age children to the bombardment by scud missiles.' *Journal of Abnormal Psychology 102,* 404–410.

Shilo-Cohen, N. (1993) 'Israeli children paint war.' In L.A. Leavitt and N.A. Fox (eds) *The Psychological Effects of War and Violence on Children.* Hillsdale, NJ: Erlbaum Associates.

Solomon, Z. (1995) *Coping with War-induced Stress.* New York: Plenum Press.

Young, J. (ed) (1996) *Saga: Best New Writings on Mythology, Volume 1.* Ashland, OR: White Cloud Press.

Ziv, A. and Israeli, R. (1973) 'Effect of bombardment on the manifest anxiety level of children living in Kibbutzim.' *Journal of Consulting and Clinical Psychology 40,* 1.

CHAPTER 4

Building Trust

Introduction

Foundational to relational, organizational, familial, group development is the necessary process of building trust. This essential building block is necessary and conditional to change at any level. In community peer support programs building trust is multifaceted. Trust issues are explored between peers themselves, peers and facilitators and the building relationship to the creative process and the holding environment. In addition, trust building is ongoing between the facilitators, the administration and other organizational collaborators. Central to trust building is the ability to be open to exploring relational, cultural and perceptual differences, setting judgment aside. Timing of establishing trust within the group setting is highly unpredictable. Most frequently within group settings trust can be highly variable with each member of the group. Even when trust has been experienced, events within or outside of the group may result in a regressive move back to an earlier phase. Modeling a tone of acceptance and mindful practices sets the stage for trust building. Creating repetitive structures such as opening rituals, building group rules, eating rituals, birthday and holiday celebrations, personal stories and sharing, and closing activities begin to form group norms. Such patterns and structures establish and maintain a sense of safety. The regularity of such practices also provides the space and opportunity for deeper exploration and sharing. This chapter will explore the paramount importance of establishing safety, trust and support within group settings.

The reader will become more familiar with how children master and integrate their highly complex feelings surrounding trauma and loss. At the same time we wish to illustrate community-based programs including the Center for Grieving Children's Multicultural Program; America's Camp, a camp designed to work with children whose parents and relatives died in the horrible events of 11 September 2001; Creating New Identities in the Work Place, a program built around the self-esteem needs of welfare recipients and their children; and clinical case examples that validate both approach and context. Whichever program is illustrated, the starting point is always the same. Building trust and developing relationships represents the essential foundation in every group formation.

Relevant theories

Traumatic events are extraordinary because they have the potential to over-whelm human adaptations and "generally involve threats to life or bodily integrity, or a close encounter with violence and death" (Herman 1992, p.33). The Diagnostic and Statistical Manual of Mental Disorders, Fourth Edition (American Psychiatric Association 1994) characterized Post Trau-matic Stress Disorder (PTSD) as a reaction to experiencing, witnessing, or confronting events that involve actual or threatened death, serious injury, or threat to the physical integrity of self or others. *The Comprehensive Textbook of Psychiatry* notes that psychological trauma is a feeling of "intense fear, help-lessness, loss of control and threat of annihilation" (Andreason 1985, p.924) from experiences that include being taken by surprise, feeling trapped, and being exposed to danger to the point of exhaustion (Green *et al.* 1990).

Western approaches to the study of trauma in children begin with defini-tions and use natural disaster samples or samples of people experiencing violence in families or communities (Mishne 2001; Whittlesey *et al.* 1999). Many recent articles use categorical analyses of PTSD, as in the Diagnostic and Statistical Manual of Mental Disorders (American Psychiatric Associa-tion 1994). This approach has also been applied to refugee children in articles by Servan-Schreiber, Lelin and Birmaher (1998) and Hyman, Beiser, and Vu (2000). They found documentation of the elevated risk of mental health problems among refugee children.

The strength of this approach lies in its cultural specificity in description and prescriptive strategies for those working with these populations. What is missing, however, is a more focused examination of the context of the trauma from those directly involved. It is possible that western scientists apply a lens to the issue, using their own normative experiences and expecta-tions for children. An increasing awareness of PTSD argues the need for early intervention as a preventative measure (Petzold 1997) and stresses people's recovery potential.

In addition, much has been written about multicultural practice in social work and the need for competence in working with people from whom one is different. We live in a multiethnic, multiracial, multiclass society. As social workers, we work with people who represent every subgroup or identity imaginable (Goldberg 2000). According to Laird (1998) we need to adopt a postmodern view of cross-cultural practice. By highlighting the continually changing and evolving nature of cultural identities, Laird and others who write from this perspective encourage us to engage in an ongoing process of learning about others and to operate as much as possible from a "not-knowing" position (Anderson and Goolishian 1992).

Dean (2001), however, goes on to assert that it is very difficult to separate ourselves from our own cultural baggage. Rather, it is more important to become aware of it and by keeping this awareness in the forefront of consciousness, it makes it more likely that we will limit its impact on our work. Our task as clinicians is to sift through and sort out different impressions, layers of meanings and awareness as we concurrently learn about others and ourselves.

Play and art therapy have been shown to provide the traumatized child with the opportunity to restructure traumatic events to provide them with meaning, to gain control over such events, and to gain a sense of control or psychological safety (Frick-Helms 1997). The literature suggests a variety of interventions which are effective for children who have lost a loved one (Webb 1993). Play therapy is one possible intervention for children experiencing loss, and the playroom can be a safe environment in which to express grief. Play represents childrens attempts to organize their experiences and their world (Landreth 1991). Children are much more likely to be comfortable using toys and play, as opposed to language, to express themselves and to show how they feel about people and events (Kottman 1995). According to Landreth, the process of play can provide the opportunity for the child to experience control even though the reality of his or her circumstances may dictate otherwise. Play involves the child's physical, emotional, and mental self in creative expression (Landreth 1991). Children use metaphorical devices to separate play from reality until the reality is bearable (Frick-Helms 1997). Moustakas (1959) noted that in the case of the disturbed child, it is his or her way of reacting to the situation and to the therapist that enables him or her to work through attitudes and to reorganize them. The result is that through play the child gains a better understanding of himself or herself as a person and a better understanding of the reality of the world. The expression of emotion and acceptance of feelings, which can occur in play, helps the child develop a personal understanding of loss. Play is pleasurable. Play is spontaneous and voluntary. Play has no extrinsic goals but instead its motivations are intrinsic by nature. Play is an inherently active engagement (Garvey 1977).

Winnicott (1971) talks about the importance of play as the ability to discover a personal means of control over what is outside one's self; to control what is outside, one has to do things, not simply to think or to wish. And doing things takes time. Playing is doing. Winnicott goes on to talk about the importance of play. "In other words, it is play that is the universal, and that belongs to health: playing leads into group relationships; playing can be a form of communication; and, lastly, playing is in the service of communication with oneself and others" (Winnicott 1971, p.41).

Other effective interventions include group play therapy and age-specific grief support groups. Children can benefit from the opportunity to share their experiences and feelings with others who are grieving. Levine and Noell (1995) suggest that the grief group creates a safe place for children to remember, share, express hurt, and begin the process of healing. Through participation in a group, children can reduce their feelings of being different, and they can have their experiences validated.

Art materials are usually part of the playroom (Landreth 1991). Use of art in play therapy is widely accepted as a means of facilitating affective expression in children. Also, art is a play medium that is particularly suitable for use with children as a beneficial and significant opportunity for their personal growth and fulfillment: creating artwork offers a form of self-expression that may be cathartic, revealing, meaningful, and therapeutically beneficial (Nickerson 1983). Naumberg (1984) stated that the individual's most fundamental thoughts and feelings reach for expression in images rather than words. Children's drawings are recordings of their vitality and life, not only the art itself but also its symbolic reference to events and objects in the world of the child. Artistic expression can be a metaphorical message translated into tangible physical terms: the child translates images and feelings into movements of shapes and colors in a shared experience with the facilitator (Mills and Crowley, 1986).

However, art therapy derives from a specific set of cultural assumptions, values, and constructions that are uniquely Euro-American in origin. Art therapy, like many activities, systems and institutions in the United States reflects the privileges of the dominant culture and perpetuates a particular "cultural worldview" (Ibrahim 1991, p.13). Many people from Asian, African and Middle Eastern backgrounds have been found to prefer a more verbal, directed, authoritative style of therapy, with clear and explicit applications to the presenting problem (Samuda and Wolfgang 1985).

Interpretation for assessment, therapeutic, or research purposes with individuals in other cultures requires substantial checks on validity and on openness to discovering the insider perspective, that is the perspective that derives from within the particular community or culture (Wells *et al.* 1995).

Researchers have consistently indicated that despite divergent cultural backgrounds, nearly all refugees encounter similar kinds of resettlement difficulties (Beiser, Turner and Ganesan 1989; Burvill 1973; Cervantes, Salgado de Snyder and Padilla 1989; Farias 1991). These common stresses of cross-cultural adaptation may be exhibited through unresolved grief, intergenerational conflict, and various psychological and behavioral manifestations of distress. Fantino and Colak (2001) identified some specific characteristics affecting the adaptation of refugee children versus immigrant children, which is an important difference for child welfare workers. They noted the hardship and violence that refugee children typically experience. They also noted that immigrants could envision the possibility of returning to their countries, whereas refugees cannot. Fantino and Colak (2001) suggested it is natural that refugee children mourn the losses of country and family. An important point is that for refugee children, grieving is often less recognized. They posited that this is due to the long-held belief that children adapt quickly and to the tendency of children not to express their sadness and their mourning in words.

Fantino and Colak (2001) also suggested that although refugee children may not know the concept of being homesick, they feel it. Some will not talk about their experiences. They suggested that perhaps many children do not talk because families or practitioners do not listen or understand how children are trying to communicate. According to Fantino and Colak (2001), in helping refugee children mourn the massive losses they have suffered, it is important to recognize the absence of prescribed rituals for healing as well as the absence of social support for the collective experience of a group of scattered people. In addition, families and child welfare workers may be so busy assisting in adjustment that they do not or cannot give children permission to grieve.

Helping children express grief

Communication barriers erected by grieving children delay problem resolution. Use of expressive arts, music, art and body movement in symbolic communication helps them to express overwhelming feelings and cope with trauma and stress. Children must be helped to "name" and "claim" these painful feelings so that they can move toward problem resolution (Segal 1984, p.590).

Children often:

- deny the existence of the traumatic event

- feel guilt because they perceive that they are personally connected to the tragedy

- internalize or act out their anger about the catastrophe

- withdraw or isolate themselves from the stressful environment

- repress their feelings about the shock

- become obsessed with the fear that the remaining parent may also die or leave

- seek spiritual comfort in the thought that the dead parent or relative is somewhere in heaven and can be communicated with through prayer

- feel confused about the cause of the relative's death or separation because the facts related to the traumatic event have not been explained to them

- become increasingly dependent upon the remaining parent

- develop a closer relationship with an existing sibling or friend as a means of gaining emotional support.

Children often experience guilt, withdrawal, denial and anger. A typical reaction is that children are frequently unable to directly communicate such feelings and concerns through verbal communication. Even when friends or family members reach out to them, it is often impossible to verbalize such complex and painful feelings. Such withdrawal and difficulty with interpersonal and social communication further exacerbates and delays the grieving process.

Children are often greatly affected by their level of cognitive and social development. Three to six-year-olds may not understand the permanence of death. As they develop abstract reasoning and comprehend the finality of death, they often become newly traumatized and impacted. When children are confronted with their own impending death or traumatic event that is extreme, they will often shut down. This is especially true when the adults in their environment are unable to express their feelings or communicate the nature of the death. Often children will protect their own parents by refusing to communicate. The trauma of death often results in loneliness and complicated feelings for children. Clark Moustakas, play therapist, cites such complications:

> Feelings of loneliness must often be hidden in childhood. They are too frightening and disturbing like any intense, severe, disturbing emotion. These feelings must be curbed, controlled or denied, or, if expressed, quickly resolved or eliminated through busy activities and goals. Children become afraid early to let others know how they actually feel. The natural and inevitable loneliness resulting in childhood must be distorted and controlled in interactions with others. The child soon believes that he can show...only expurgated, carefully edited versions of his inner life. (Moustakas 1961, p.40).

Children often feel a sense of hopelessness and rely on the primary defenses of grief, denial, withdrawal and repression in order to deal with their loss and grief. Depression and accompanying feelings of guilt and worthlessness can dominate their moods. Anger is often misunderstood. It is normal for children to feel unresolved feelings of abandonment, outrage and unexpressed anger at the loss of a parent or relative.

Abne M. Eisenberg and Ralph R. Smith reported about the significance of symbolic communication. Underlying feelings and needs are acted out non-verbally. Emotions are easily put into action. Eisenberg and Smith attest to the fact that a large part of interpersonal communication is expressed non-verbally (Eisenberg and Smith 1971).

Children's art in the Holocaust

Children's art in the concentration camps of the Holocaust was done in secret and then hidden; it has become part of the "clandestine art" of the Holocaust (Costanza 1982). Costanza noted that there was something bizarre in many of the artworks of such children, such as the presence of discomforting elements: unnatural and oversized forms replaced the child, who is usually the largest shape in children's drawings; death images appeared in many of the works; and, in one case, an entire page was smudged by a sooty gray. In these drawings, faces rarely smile, and oversized tears flow from little eyes to make an inadvertent pattern over the entire page. Black strokes from odd-sized chimneys dissect these blue and green child landscapes.

After the war, two suitcases filled with paintings, poems, and drawings were found at Terezin and at other camps; these artifacts are now housed in several Holocaust museums and have been copied and printed in various publications. Many of these surviving pictures from Terezin are scenes of frolic in playgrounds despite the fact that no real playgrounds existed in the camp. To engage in the kind of play shown in the drawings, the children's imaginations had to transcend the barbed wire fences. These pictures are interesting in the wish they express to carry the unfortunate children back to a happier time and place. Eisen (1988) held that it was as if the children could not reflect on the immediate present but only a fantasy world where anything could happen.

When Gerald Green (1969), in his book *The Artists of Terezin*, writes about the remarkable culture that flourished in a concentration camp in Czechoslovakia, he emphasizes how adults as well as children turned to art, poetry, and philosophy as a means of both recording their plight and retaining their humanity. When forty pounds of goods was all that Jews were able to bring for personal belongings, they chose to carry art supplies, musical instruments, and books. Whenever possible these creative tools both offered light during an incredibly dark struggle and offered solace for the hearts and souls of the community.

In summary, the therapeutic value of art ranges across a continuum from art as a projective technique providing a view of the child's inner world to art as a vehicle for facilitating expression, movement and growth (Allan 1988; Furth 1988). Some of the basic principles of the therapeutic relationship were seen in the approach of Friedl Dicker-Brandeis in her work with children. The critical importance of the establishment of a trusting relationship was noted by Makarova (1990) as one of the important elements of Dicker-Brandeis' work. Her compassion and tender attitude, and the love that the children had for her are also considered important therapeutic factors in her work. The value of play and art in the lives of children, particularly in a world of fear and death, is validated by the experience of the children of Terezin. The value of the relationship, as exemplified by Dicker-Brandeis, normalized and restored the continuity of the children's life within her art class. It is the relationship that is the critical element of play, survival, and healing. It was said of Dicker-Brandeis that her work in the camp was the culmination of her lifelong endeavor in that it was there that she helped hundreds of children to find genuine human wealth in the inhuman condition of their existence in a concentration camp.

What cannot be put into words clearly lives in the heart, soul and body of mankind. Grounding ourselves in such realities means providing unconditional loving support and nourishment. Such conditions build trust in significant and exponential ways.

Building trust

The Multicultural Program at the Center for Grieving Children is action centered and focuses on a safe way to hold children from diverse backgrounds while offering them free choices to express their feelings and underlying stories. Body-centered activities include expressive arts activities, physical movement, music, action-oriented games, dramatic play activities, story telling, and organizing a scrapbook representing the journey from their homeland to their present family home. Children have the opportunity to use the Volcano Room, which is set up with boxing gloves, mats, boxing bag, foam noodles, and fun equipment. The ground rules are simple. Children are asked to maintain eye contact, to finish what they start, and not to hurt themselves or others. Children can freely access and express any feelings that they wish in an open studio with a rich selection of art materials, projects, a personal scrapbook, two and three-dimensional art activities and games that take children further into the expression and the release of experiences having to do with their present situation, the past and their imagined future.

Following are examples from the Multicultural Program and other programs that illustrate how the issues of trust are interwoven through interpersonal relationships, art expressions, behaviors and actions.

Children's stories

In a group of middle-school-age boys from the Sudan and Somalia, difficulties in building trust emerge. Facilitators realize that the boys are unable to safely express their separate feeling states as they individually and collectively dart from the group room into the hall and adjoining spaces. After many attempts to regain the membership, a game format was chosen by the facilitators. Pretending to play a game of hide and seek, each facilitator greeted the runners as if they had been re-discovered.

Expressions of surprise, excitement and fun were experienced as each were invited back to the group room. More trust emerged and a discussion ensued about the game of hide and seek. As a group the boys volunteered playing the game as they remembered it in the Sudan and Somalia. The new hide and seek game had rules that the boys created. All games were played inside the group room. The lights were put out and each person had to be found and touched. The first person touched would lead the count and be the next leader of the game. This game became the trust-building process of the group and was often chosen as the opening ritual for group meetings.

Working with the same group of pre-adolescent boys, a group facilitator discusses a way to bring the boys together in a group-building process. A discussion emerges whereby the facilitators and the children talk about card games that have been played in this culture and in their culture of origin. A fun game is devised whereby sports playing cards are placed leaning vertically and horizontally against the wall. Each member of the group could use one of their own cards to throw from a group-defined line to try to knock over the cards against the wall. One by one the playing cards were thrown and whenever some of the cards against the wall fell, the player could add them to his own deck. Lots of verbal expression of anger, and ultimate joy burst from the boys' mouths as they tried various hand techniques in throwing their cards. Ultimate winners could hold their winnings or share as they willed. The generosity and group support and spirit was palpable as the game provided an excellent arena to build support and trust within the group. Some of the group members hoarded their cards while others noticed those without and began to share. Sharing did not go unnoticed as members receiving the cards gave many thanks. Soon such peer support became part of the game practice. Open sharing improved a sense of trust within the group.

In a creative group process an eleven-year-old Somalian boy crafts a beaded bracelet connected to a yellow cut-out shape (figure 4.1). He then offers this treasure to the female facilitator of the group. At a symbolic level the yellow cut-out is in the shape of his homeland of Somalia. At a non-verbal level this boy's creativity speaks both to the building of trust and connections within the group and to the continued inner feelings and connections to his homeland of Somalia.

Figure 4.1: Beaded bracelet

A young Sudanese girl expressed both in body language and facial expression her resistance to move from her opening circle to her small focused group. When her facilitator and peers tried to understand her behavior she remained non-verbal. At one point her peer group decided to make pizza and to share this with other peers. The facilitators had introduced knitting which became a favorite activity that supported positive peer interaction and communication. As knitting became a group ritual this young girl sabotaged the process by making a negative comment to one of the facilitators. The facilitator voiced how these words affected her and suggested that maybe something deeper was going on. Leaving the room, the girl reflected on her feelings and actions. Peers and facilitators encouraged her to come back, upon which she wholeheartedly apologized to everyone in the room. From that moment forward she was not only able to rejoin the group but also was able to express her feelings without her old behaviors. She was able to ask the group for support during a period of time when her mother went to visit family in the Sudan. Her request spurred other group members to recall their own stories and journeys regarding transition and loss. The element of trust became more palpable as her behavior and resistance were accepted and clarified rather than being judged. Steady support from both the facilitators and peers created a higher level of trust within the group.

The Tornado Room

One facilitator of the Tornado Room shares her perceptions of how children release chaotic, aggressive, and angry feelings through physical activity. The room is small, roughly eight by ten feet in size, and is covered in red padding with a large black punching bag in the center. Some call it the Volcano Room, some the Tornado Room, and she preferred the Room of Truth. As children were given permission to express feelings safely through their body without judgment, expressions of anger as well as quietness would emerge. Many times the observation was that as children expressed themselves aggressively by hitting the bag with boxing gloves, using foam bats, hitting the wall with foam noodles or their feet, they screamed and would often cry as their sadness emerged. There were times that their individual culture emerged as they would perform ritual dances or sing in their native tongue. Such feelings expressed through their bodies continue to affirm the building of trust.

America's Camp

Located on a hillside overlooking Lake Mah-Kee-Nac in Lenox, Massachusetts, America's Camp is a camp funded by the America's Camp Foundation and devoted to supporting the children whose parents and relatives were killed in the horrible events of 11 September 2001. This camp is in its fifth year of operation. Over 230 children attend. Camp counselors come from other camps as volunteers. These counselors reflect a high level of excellence, devotion and diversity. Counselors come from all over the world. Over 22 adolescents are Counselors in Training (CITs). These adolescents were previously campers who now volunteer their support to younger camp participants. Richly supported, America's Camp has senior counselors, grief counselors, an artist in residence, a spiritual director, administrators, nurses and other support staff.

The primary mission of America's Camp is to provide children with a fun-filled rich camping experience that embraces their peer and developmental needs along with direct support and collaboration regarding their grief. The Center for Grieving Children provides consultation and direct support with a facility known as Buddy Central. Campers are free to utilize Buddy Central on an individual and group basis. Mental health consultants along with the Center's facilitators provide direct services to counselors and other camp staff.

Bob Ditter, a licensed clinical social worker and on-site consultant, educator to America's Camp, describes witnessing what Judith Harris (1998), in her book entitled *The Nurture Assumption*, described as the salient factor, a well-known concept in social psychology. Bob, in his article "Lessons learned, we are not alone" (Ditter 2003), goes on to explain that the most powerful salient factor in America's Camp is that every child has lost a parent. When children recognize that their peers have had similar experiences then the peer group becomes a strong positive influence and connection. Children do not want to be seen as different and singled out. The salient factor rings true as it is easy for children to share stories about their mother or father, and compare facts with other children about what engine company their dad was from or where they were when they first heard about the tragedy, or how hard children still struggle to remember their parent's face or the sound of their parent's voice. Such connections resound with building elements of trust both for individuals as well as the camp itself.

Yearly the re-connection with the peer group, the camp facility, counselors and support staff rekindles a sense of safety, trust and well-being. When camp begins bus loads of children come from Boston, New York, New Jersey and other New England states. Counselors are sent out to greet children and their families and join the children on the journey to camp. Cell phone communication is established between the buses and camp. A countdown takes place at camp with announcements of the timing of the children's arrival. All counselors and staff line the entry roads. When the buses arrive emotions are high and the children feel the support, love and re-connections. Such opening rituals build on a sense of trust and connection.

Many children arrive at camp to be greeted by familiar faces and known counselors. Settling into their cabins, familiar and new friendships are established. The rituals of life in the cabins such as wake-up calls, meals, structured activities, sharing circles, Buddy Central, outings, begin to create a safe and predictable structure through which trust evolves. In addition the community art project, dining hall activities which include singing and dancing, and structured sports and outdoor activities set the stage for peer and staff connections which enable building trust at various levels.

Creating New Identities in the Work Place

In collaboration with the Maine Additional Support for People in Retraining and Employment (ASPIRE) Program, Work Opportunities Unlimited, Department of Health and Human Services (DHHS), and the Children's Cabinet, comprising of case management supervisors and specialist and DHHS case managers, a twelve-week peer support program was established. The program resulted in participants not only getting to tell their life stories and be heard, but also more importantly getting to re-discover the roots of their own resiliency. The twelve-week group process explored both the pain and resiliency of ASPIRE welfare recipients who have tremendous barriers to employment and feeling successful in the world. Each participant also worked with a work opportunities unlimited career resource specialist (CRS) for job development and for job placement. There was good communication between the CRS and group facilitators to support each participant's progress.

Resiliency theories often purport to the abilities of children to navigate through the complex issues of trauma and recovery. Seldom do we consider the application of such theories to adult life situations. Most of the group participants were parents of children. Barriers such as the need for childcare, for child therapeutic and medical services and for daycare loom large as obstacles to employment opportunities. Children are top priorities in these parents' lives. Through peer support, mindful exercises, guided imagery, creative expression, decision-making trees, and problem solving with the Children's Cabinet, many of these obstacles were resolved. Coupled with these barriers, every parent wished for opportunities regarding the welfare of their children. In review of each adult's life story one could observe both the barriers and opportunities that were embedded in the relational fabric of their life events.

Central to building trust within these groups have been the self-reflective activities of creating a life story based on the ways in which each member has survived various times in their own life span development. Autobiographical stories were developed by using time lines and a clock face as a way of drawing and illustrating various times in life development as well as significant life experiences. Although difficult transitions appear in both the drawings and the resulting narratives, participants were asked to stay focused on how they persevered through such times. Focusing on underlying positive attributes and positive possibilities becomes the essential building block in creating trust and acceptance. Most group participants have been involved in endless groups and programs focused on deficits and problematic behaviors and practices. Exploring the notion that within themselves are the insights and answers for their most problematic issues opens the door for building a higher level of trust. As each group member shared their personal stories and gave witness to the stories of others there grew a significant number of connecting themes and familiar life experiences. Such connections enabled participants to increase their level of trust and to take further risks in being open to change.

Group members have been disengaged from work experiences as well as community involvement for significant amounts of time. For many there is an accumulation of negative myths about how antagonistic the work place can be. Because of multiple levels of trauma and anxiety participants have few sources of encouragement. Creating a safe place where such tragedy can be explored and empathically honored creates opportunities to investigate the possibility for building trust and hope.

One woman comes to a group meeting with a tragic story of not being able to get support from her adult daughter, friends, nor from her birth family including neither of her parents. Crying, she reveals her dilemma to the group. Before group members responded, a facilitator asked what she was doing for herself regarding the impossibility of the situation. She replied that the only thing that seemed to help was prayer. Other group members recalled times in their own lives when such despair and loss was omnipresent. Many participants volunteered how they themselves had turned to prayer to resolve conflict and despair. One group member talked about the fact that prayer surrounds you with positive energy when hope seems impossible. Another group member declared that prayer creates the space where something positive might happen. Insights from various group members created an atmosphere of trust and well-being.

Conclusion

The Multicultural Program, America's Camp and the group process for Creating New Identities in the Work Place create a safe place for individuals to explore the collective reality of their pain, trauma and loss. Within each group setting the structures, rituals, practices and strength-based philosophy build a stronger sense of safety, trust and well-being. Peer support in each program underlies the importance of both releasing and resolving conflict in communities of peers that share common experiences.

In a parallel process facilitators and participants alike are encouraged to be present with their feelings and perceptions. As a result a high level of peer support and trust is built whereby the past, present and future can be addressed at any moment. Trauma and past conflicts continue to be triggered in present situations. Manifest in family life and social experience are underlying repressed fears, anxieties and conflicts that are being constantly replayed. Facilitators need to make such encounters available and observable by promoting awareness. Peer support models ultimately encourage participants to deepen their awareness of themselves and to process that awareness within a supportive community that ultimately accepts and grounds such feelings and perceptions. Never alone, facilitators and peers become witnesses that affirm and when needed share and join in the pain and joy of such exploration. In an attempt to deepen the process, facilitators are often confronted with the emotional power that such exploration unleashes. Developing safe and trustworthy patterns, rituals and consistent responses to deeper listening are essential in supporting the confidence that group members need in building trust.

Creating a safe environment and strengthening feelings of safety and trust must take priority. The most widely used and apparently effective approaches are programs that provide reassurance and support while gradually, often indirectly, exploring the often traumatic past. As a result participants are helped to gradually uncover traumatic history, to make sense of overwhelming experiences and to identify and express underlying affect necessary for healing to take place. Creating a safe place for such processing, the Multicultural Program engages the children in art-based activities along with the Tornado Room. America's Camp has many venues where children can feel safe while they do art and process the feelings and thoughts that are generated from it. "Buddy Central" is one such safe place where grief facilitators are available to support arts and crafts exploration along with structured games, the Tornado Room and spontaneous discussion. Camp bunk houses become a safe place where peers can share openly with their counselors and with each other. The community-based art program is yet another safe place where highly creative and often emotional communication is encouraged and supported.

Within the group process for Creating New Identities in the Work Place, opening rituals included readings from *Small Graces* by Kent Nerburn (1998). These rituals helped the group to build a sense of trust and safety.

Creating safety and building trust is well illustrated in fairy tales and myth literature by the lead characters who feel compelled to go on a journey or quest that is often not of their choice. In the tale of Cinderella she established her safety and trust by creating a daily ritual by going to her mother's grave. Cinderella's stepmother and stepsisters often made her feel like an outcast. She was forced to find a way out of her entrapment. Cinderella trusted that her father would break off the first twig that touched his hat on his way home from the fair. The hazel twig grew into a tree from Cinderella's tears which were shed daily at her mother's grave. Soon the birds on the hazel tree magically empower Cinderella to get what she wished for. This daily ritual is resplendent with all of the ingredients necessary for building safety and trust.

Building trust and safety can quickly move to the expression of anger, fear and conflict as individuals often express underlying affect associated with the trauma itself or with the defenses built around re-entering such pain. Such conflict often blocks spontaneity and movement to the past or forward to the future.

References

Allan, J. (1988) *Inscapes of the Child's World: Jungian Counseling in Schools and Clinics.* Dallas: TX Spring Publications.

American Psychiatric Association (1994) Desk reference to the diagnostic criteria from DSM-IV. Washington, DC: American Psychiatric Association.

Anderson, H. and Goolishian, H. (1992) 'The client is the expert: a not-knowing approach to therapy' In S. McNamee and K.J. Gergen (eds) *Therapy as Social Construction.* London, Sage Publications.

Andreason, N. (1985) 'Post-traumatic stress disorder.' In H.I. Kaplan and B.J. Sadock (eds) *Comprehensive Textbook of Psychiatry.* Fourth edition. Baltimore, MD: Williams and Wilkins.

Beiser, M., Turner, R.J. and Ganesan, S. (1989) 'Catastrophic stress and factors affecting its consequences among Southeast Asian refugees.' *Social Science and Medicine 28*, 3, 183–195.

Burvill, P.W. (1973) 'Immigration and mental disease.' *Australian and New Zealand Journal of Psychiatry 7*, 3 September, 155–162.

Cervantes, R. C., Salgado de Snyder, V. N. and Padilla, A. M. (1989) 'Posttraumatic stress in immigrants from Central America and Mexico.' *Hospital and Community Psychiatry 40*, 615–619.

Costanza, M. S. (1982) *The Living Witness: Art in the Concentration Camps and Ghettos.* New York: Free Press.

Dean, R. G. (2001) 'The myth of cross-cultural competence.' *Families in Society 82*, 623–630.

Dicker-Brandeis, F. (1988) Friedl Dicker-Brandeis: 1898–1944 exhibition to commemorate the 90th anniversary of her birthday. Prague, State Jewish Museum.

Dicker-Brandeis, F. Kinderzeichenen. Jerusalem, Israel, the Central Archives for the Disaster and the Heroism, Yad-Washem.

Ditter, B. (2003) 'Lessons learned, we are not alone.' *Camping Magazine 76*, 1, 26–31.

Eisen, G. (1988) *Children and Play in the Holocaust: Games Among the Shadows.* Amherst, MA: University of Massachusetts Press.

Eisenberg, A.M. and Smith R.R. Jr. (1971) *Non-Verbal Communication.* New York: Bobs Merrill.

Fantino, A.M. and Colak, A. (2001) 'Refugee children in Canada: searching for identity.' *Child Welfare 80*, 5, September/October, 587–596.

Farias, P.J. (1991) 'Emotional stress and its socio-political correlates in Salvadoran refugees: analysis of a clinical sample.' *Culture, Medicine and Psychiatry 15*, 167–192.

Frick-Helms, S. (1997) 'Boys cry better than girls: play therapy behaviors of children residing in a shelter for battered women.' *International Journal of Play Therapy 6*, 73–91.

Furth, G.M. (1988) *The Secret World of Drawings: Healing Through Art.* Boston, MA: Sigo Press.

Garvey, C. (1977) *Play.* Cambridge, MA: Harvard University Press.

Goldberg, M. (2000) 'Conflicting principles in multicultural social work.' *Families in Society 81*, 12–21.

Green, B., Lindy, J., Grace, M., Gleser and Gross G. (1990) 'Buffalo Creek survivors in the second decade: stability of stress symptoms.' *American Journal of Orthopsychiatry 60*, 1, 43–54.

Green, G. (1969) *The Artists of Terezin.* New York: Hawthorn Books.

Harris, J. (1998) *The Nuture Assumption: Why Children Turn Out the Way They Do.* New York: Free Press.

Herman, J. (1992) *Trauma and Recovery.* New York: Basic Books.

Hyman, I., Beiser, M. and Vu, N. (2000) 'Post-migration stresses among Southeast Asian refugee youth in Canada: universal, culture-specific and situational.' *Journal of Comparative Family Studies 31*, 2, 281–294.

Ibrahim, F. (1991) 'Contribution of cultural worldview to generic counseling and development.' *Journal of Counseling and Development 70*, 13–19.

Kottman, T. (1995) *Partners in Play: An Adlerian Approach to Play Therapy.* Alexandria, VA: American Counseling Association.

Laird, J. (1998) 'Theorizing culture: narrative ideas and practice principles.' In M. McGoldrick (ed) *Revisioning Family Therapy.* New York: Guilford.

Landreth, G. L. (1991) *Play Therapy: The Art of the Relationship.* Muncie, IN: Accelerated Development Press.

Levine, J. and Noell, D. (1995) 'Embracing fears and sharing tears: working with grieving children.' In S. Smith and M. Pennells (eds) *Interventions with Bereaved Children.* Bristol, PA: Kingsley.

Makarova, E. (1990) *From Bauhaus to Terezin: Friedl Dicker-Brandeis and her Pupils.* Jerusalem, Israel, Holocaust Martyrs' and Heroes' Remembrance Authority, The Art Museum.

Mills, J. and Crowley, R. (1986) *Therapeutic Metaphors for Children and the Child Within.* New York: Brunner/Mazel.

Mishne, J. (2001) 'Psychological trauma in adolescence: familial disillusionment and loss of personal identity.' *American Journal of Psychoanalysis 61*, 1, March, 63–84.

Moustakas, C. (1959) *Psychotherapy with Children.* New York: Ballantine Books.

Moustakas, C (1961) *Loneliness.* Englewood Cliffs, NJ: Prentice Hall.

Naumberg (1984) 'Introduction.' In T. Dalley (ed) *Art as Therapy: An Introduction to the Use of Art as a Therapeutic Technique.* New York, Tavistock Routledge.

Nerburn, K. (1998) *Small Graces.* Novato, CA: New World Library.

Nickerson, E.T. (1983) 'Art as a play therapeutic medium.' In C.E. Schaefer, and K.J. O'Connor (eds) *Handbook of Play Therapy.* New York: John Wiley.

Petzold, H. (1997) 'The treatment of post traumatic stress disorders.' In Fourth European Arts Therapies Conference, September 12–15, 1997, London.

Samuda, R.J. and Wolfgang, A. (eds) (1985) *Intercultural Counseling and Assessment: Global Perspective.* New York: C.J. Hogrefe.

Segal, R.M. (1984) 'Helping children express grief through symbolic communication.' *Social Casework: The Journal of Contemporary Social Work.* December, 590–599.

Servan-Schreiber, D., Lelin, B. and Birmaher, B. (1998) 'Post-traumatic stress disorder and major depressive disorder in Tibetan refugee children.' *Journal of the American Academy of Child and Adolescent Psychiatry 37*, 874–879.

Webb, N.B. (1993) 'Counseling and therapy for the bereaved child.' In N.B. Webb (ed) *Helping Bereaved Children.* New York: Guilford.

Wells, A. M., Hirshberg, D., Lipton, M. and Oakes, J. (1995) 'Bounding the case within its context: a constructivist approach to studying detracking reform.' *Educational Researcher 24*, 5, 18–24.

Whittlesey, S.W., Allen, J.R., Bell, B.D., Lindsey, E.D., Speed, L.F., Lucas, A.F., Ware, M.M., Allen, S.F. and Pfefferbaum, B. (1999) 'Avoidance in trauma: conscious and unconscious defense, pathology and health.' *Psychiatry 62*, 4, 303–312.

Winnicott, D.W. (1971) *Playing and Reality.* New York: Basic Books.

CHAPTER 5

Anger, Fear and Conflict

Introduction

Just when trust and safety have been established, one expects to experience the outpouring of insight and self-acceptance: perhaps, at least, a personal epiphany or awareness. Instead the path is highly individualized and unpredictable. Anger, fear and conflict are very often the first emotions that rise with both intensity and purpose. Such feelings act as a form of release as higher levels of trust take away the need for control and containment. Defenses such as denial, repression, and intellectualization give way when individuals access deeper levels of awareness through creative expression and group involvement. Spontaneous activities and expressions remain unfiltered and therefore more succinct with underlying affects and needs. Quite often the complexity of trauma and loss has forbidden the necessary expression of rage, anger and fundamental vulnerability. Distrust is experienced internally as well as socially. Unpredictable feelings are unleashed that may be the precursor to unresolved grief. Resistance and a high level of reactivity may become the norm.

Supporting participants to engage in pleasurable and creative processes with the arts and with physical movement, play and activity, is the antithesis of the control and limits that the defenses provide for protection. In other words, to the extent that group members have been traumatized, there is a parallel process whereby their inability to engage in the direct expression of their pain and loss is also reflected in their ability to embrace joy and pleasure. Inhibited by the traumatic events and the resulting impact, many individuals are less available for play, art, or any free movement whereby they avoid the possibility of triggering feelings connected to the fearful events and circumstances.

In this chapter we will explore the uncovering of underlying affects as they are expressed in the action processes and explorations within various group settings. The Multicultural Program, America's Camp, Creating New Identities in the Work Place; each reveal this necessary step in the healing process. Exemplary of the need to move beyond natural defenses, the outward expression of anger, disappointment and outrage are essential in re-creating safety and acknowledging the essential truth.

Multicultural Program

In a community collaboration with the Portland Museum of Art, the photography exhibition "Sebastião Salgado: Migrations" portrayed people and families in transition. The children were asked to do a drawing that had something to do with their journey to the United States.

A young girl from the Sudan makes many attempts to create a painting of her family in transition. After her third piece of paper she takes the paints, pours them on the surface of the paper and in a regressive moment places both hands in the paint and turns the vivid color into a muddy brown. "This is poop," she later mutters, "That's what it was like when we had to leave, I just want to forget it all!"

In a group of ten-year-old boys from the Sudan, anger breaks out. The boys take an oversized toy gorilla out of a pile of stuffed animals and begin to wrestle, fight, box, and aggressively express their anger and rage. Over several group sessions the anger and aggression progress to the point that the facilitators ask the peers to identify what is going on. With little awareness in the group, the boys become conscious that they are literally pulling the gorilla apart. One boy volunteers that his father believes that you need to be strong and physically able to fight, especially when you grow up with a war going on just outside of your home.

A co-facilitator tells the story of where the gorilla came from. She explains that the gorilla belonged to a boy who died from cancer and after his death his family donated the gorilla to the Center for other children. One by one the boys talk about how they want to repair the gorilla. They collectively decide that they will use purple thread to sew its seams together and that they will put notes in its heart before sewing it up in the next session. One boy draws the gorilla and says that he is sorry for how the boys have treated it (figure 5.1). Some boys share the contents of their notes, others slip their notes quietly into the stuffing of the gorilla. One boy says that he wishes that the men who hurt and killed his relatives could say that they were sorry.

Figure 5.1: Sorry gorilla

A whole session centers around the ritual of repairing the gorilla and the children decide that the gorilla will now sit beside one member of the group at a time as a symbol of protection and support.

In a group of boys from the Sudan a request comes up to create masks (figures 5.2, 5.3 and 5.4). The group decides that they want to work with mask forms that are hanging in other parts of the Center. The facilitators point out that these forms are white and Caucasian-looking and wonder if they would like other masks or faces that are more Afro-centric. The group decides that they prefer the white masks. In a later session the masks are being painted and decorated when members of the group suddenly become angry.

Grabbing each other's masks, peers start adding clay to the nose, lips and other features and impulsively change the features of the masks to look more Afro-centric in nature. One boy asserts that he is tired of being in a culture where very few people have dark skin or look like him or his family.

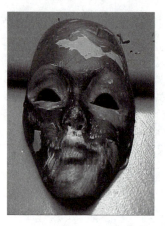

Figure 5.2: Mask 1

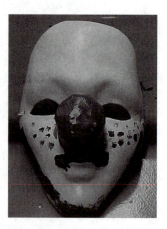

Figure 5.3: Mask 2

Figure 5.4: Mask 3

Another boy asserts that as soon as he is old enough he wants to return to the Sudan. Many boys discuss the fact that if it were not for their safety, they wouldn't want to be in this American culture at all.

Such spontaneous expressions of anger actually provide opportunity for catharsis as well as new connections to the conflicted past. In both groups, the boys were more able to make reference to the past as a part of their present experience after they had safely accessed their feelings of anger and rage without being immediately judged and curtailed.

A group of boys from the Sudan and Somalia, who were previously mentioned, transformed their anger and distrust through a game of hide and seek. Within this group the game created an atmosphere of fun and trust building. There was lots of laughter and there were no incidents of aggressive behavior. At one point block printing was introduced and the oldest Somalian boy who had not shared much about himself eagerly engaged in the process. With great effort he took a T-shirt and hand printed Somalia on one side and his home village of Buuhoodle on the opposite side. Unprecedented as an event, this was the first time that this boy had either stopped running or focused his attention on something positive and relaxing. He displayed a positive affect and engaged in the process with an in-depth notion of purpose, pride and specific stories about his family. Of particular importance was the fact that many of his family members were still in Somalia.

America's Camp

What creates more complicated grief for the children whose parents died in the events of 11 September 2001 is that their private and personal grief is constantly bombarded by the historic precedence of the event. Children watch the events on television and their feelings are re-triggered by the visual reminders from the media, television, movies and visual posters. For each of the campers these images and scenes are not the well-worn images of a past trauma but are constant, deeply intimate reminders of their parent's death. In a *New York Times* article on 11 September 2004, the following quotation was given: "It was seeing my Dad die over and over again," said Sarah Van Auken, 15, whose father Kenneth Van Auken worked at Cantor Fitzgerald.

Younger children spent endless hours in the Tornado Room at Buddy Central piling mattresses one on top of the other. During such play children would sandwich themselves between the mattresses where play foam noodles were offered as breathing tubes. Play themes moved from towers falling, to rescue attempts, to spontaneous aggression and anger over the impossibility of the situation. Frequently children would play out these scenes over and over again.

A 12-year-old boy's feelings were triggered by a camp closing event. Camp counselors and adults surrounded the children with candles while various songs were sung between the two. After the event, this 12-year-old boy withdrew from his peers and cabin counselor. It took some time and quiet encouragement but he was finally able to say that he missed his mother and was never able to see her again to say goodbye. With careful attention and empathy he was encouraged to talk about his mother and why he missed her. Crying, he actually released some of his sadness and acknowledged her importance in his life now as much as then.

Field trips are an important part of the camping experience. On one such trip to a sporting event a nine-year-old boy became immobilized and angry on the bus trip back to camp. At first he started hitting his peers. When he was asked to move to a seat with a counselor he became enraged and combative. It was impossible to calm him down and it became necessary to restrain him during the drive back. Later as his resistance diminished he was able to verbalize that his last encounter with his father was accompanying him to a sports event.

Creating New Identities in the Work Place

Jackie, in one of the support groups, came into a group meeting angry and agitated. When facilitators checked in with group members, Jackie talked about how angry she was feeling. She expanded by saying that she was angry with her case manager, but especially angry with a boyfriend who had left her. This guy, she explained, was on crack and took her car leaving her "high and dry." She stood by him and followed him through a rehab program. Despite all of her support, he left with her car and has never returned. She was able finally to locate her car but it could not be fixed. She felt that the car was necessary for transporting her adolescent daughter and for her own appointments and needs. She became very agitated and got up to leave the room. Other group members counseled with her, reinforcing that leaving was a pattern. They tried to help her consider a different choice. Finally, one group member was able to convince her to do a scribble drawing. Jackie's drawing revealed a tornado, sharks, birds, a river and a canoe. At one point Jackie's anger turned into tears and she began to relate to the group how tragic her adolescent life had been. According to Jackie she had suffered so much abuse that she ran from her home and ended up on the street homeless. Her encounters on the street did not improve her life and her ability to trust herself and others was extremely low.

Most of Jackie's adolescent and adult life was spent running from one conflict into another. For a brief moment in the group Jackie was able to stop her fight or flight response and to move through some of the anger. Other group members were able to support Jackie to be aware that there were programs like Faith Works and Good Wheels that help people in purchasing a car.

Grace from the same group shares how angry she has been about the difficult and often tragic events in her own life. Grace talks about a period in her life when she hung out with a lot of "bad people." Often walking home late at night Grace would feel fearful and anxious about the possibility of someone hurting her. As she neared a bridge close to her home she would often run in fear that someone would be hiding underneath or near the bridge. It got to the point that Grace was scared to walk across the bridge near her house at night. Grace shared early in the group that her mother had died when she was six. She also would often use the phrase, when difficulties occurred and she would pick herself up after the fall: "I don't know where I start but here I go" (figure 5.5)

David talks about how much conflict he experienced in late childhood through adolescence and adulthood (figure 5.6.) He feels strongly that his partner and their family have steered him in a positive direction. David still gets very angry at authority figures and describes situations which have led to numerous physical and verbal altercations with legal ramifications. He has felt misunderstood and poorly supported for most of his life. David recalls that one of the few exceptions was that just before his father died he had verbalized that he loved him.

Conclusion

The aforementioned stories illustrate how anger, fear and conflict initiate the healing process. When we have the opportunity to reflect back on the nature of loss and trauma it becomes clear that individuals face adversity without support, love, safety or understanding of how to navigate through such difficulty. Often caregivers are incapacitated themselves because of personal

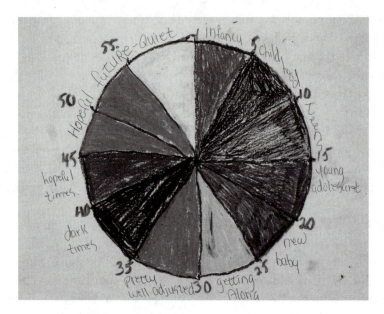

Figure 5.5: Grace's life story mandala

Figure 5.6: David's life line drawing

trauma, stress, or the repetition cycle of pain. Such impasses get recorded in the body and are easily triggered or re-activated. Once trust and safety are established uncovering the past quickly moves to the feeling states and mental states of the original impasse. Re-discovering what underlies such impasse is the journey to recovery.

Jonathan Young, Jungian psychologist, shares in his book of ancient stories, *SAGA* (Young 1996), a story from the Scriptures. During the time when the Scriptures were written it was common for women to sew valuable metallic coins to their garments. Like a dowry, the coins represented a valued possession and related possession to the familial and social status and identity of an individual. As the story goes, a woman loses the coin and devotes all her time and effort to recovering what she has lost. She lights a lamp and sweeps day and night until she finds the lost treasure. She wants her neighbors and friends to share in her relief and joyous celebration. The discovery of the coin and the ultimate celebration of its recovery, on a simple level, embodies the regaining of a lost aspect of herself or even a lost part of her soul. In much the same way parts of one's self-identity are lost or fall away and the stress is poignantly felt. The recovery process is likened to the grief process of searching for and re-discovering the image and memories that provide meaning and guide us through life. Without the opportunity to explore and reflect on what we have lost, there is no ability to treasure, integrate, or understand what gives our life meaning.

For each of the adults, children and their families, recovering what has given their lives meaning before the process of fleeing from war, running from abuse, witnessing a tragic death, losing a parent, or fleeing from danger, have become the lost elements. The human crisis and pain, the need to acculturate and adjust to western culture, the pressure to move on, the necessity to make other life decisions, removes individuals from the crisis at hand. More slow and unpredictable re-calling of past memories, losses, grief and recollections from the past go undercover yet the sweeping, or uncovering, is what continues to have meaning and purpose and is critical to healing the lost pieces of the past.

Many families and children rely on their resilience to make the necessary changes and adjustments. When given the opportunity to stop and reflect by utilizing creative and autobiographic resources, heartfelt dialogues uncover the not too distant connection and meaning of the pain that is held within.

Whatever story we explore, whether it be from the Scriptures, *The Iliad*, the Grimm's fairy tales, or other folk tales and stories, there is often a search for missing elements. Most critical to the story and to the personal enlightenment and discovery is a devotional practice, a creative process, an intentional desire, a magical belief, or a poetic sensibility.

Opening up to the images and their symbolic meaning results in a personal identification with these elements in our own lives. Stories throughout the ages impart wisdom and shed light and guidance on our human condition. In reality, precious coins and repeated stories outlast all other cultural artifacts. Coins and stories utilize imagery as sources of wisdom and insight. Stories, more than coins, are filled with symbolic imagery that we can begin to study and uncover the spiritual significance of each image.

Profoundly gifted in their ability to be present, children dare to explore the ongoing meaning of their lives by entering the world of mythic story. Over and over again children's resilience points out the plasticity of the human brain. Trusting the need to play, children enter realities that they can only imagine and therefore add meaning and give resolution to the realities that they find difficult if not impossible to integrate. Children are in fact leaders in understanding the human physiological need for movement, creativity, and self-expression as the means necessary for gaining distance and insight into what causes pain, anxiety and distrust at an inner level. As the stories in this process are told, it is also interesting to note that as children uncover the often conflictual past, they change their focus of attention to an activity or process that is calming rather than tension producing. Such pauses are notable not only in the children's play with mattresses, re-creating the floors of the Twin Towers, but also apparent in the adult's scribble drawing which helped to pause the fight or flight response.

Mythically the trials and conflicts that one encounters in the forest or throughout the journey create periodic impasse. Anger, fear and conflict, that may be interfering with deeper thinking and deeper problem solving, need to be expressed. The good and evil energies operate one after the other, making passage slow, awkward and sometimes discouraging. Such trials and tribulations are necessary before the true path can be uncovered or known.

In Hansel and Gretel, no matter how many times Hansel anticipates their fateful abandonment in the woods, his resourcefulness is ultimately challenged. Without a clear path out of the woods both Hansel and Gretel rely deeply on their inner instincts and awarenesses. Challenged by their evil stepmother, the woods, the witch, and nature itself, both children persevere by facing their fears. They often rely on signs from nature such as the white bird and the duck that ultimately help them to find their way home.

A reaction of associated feelings and cognitions related to past traumas and conflicts opens the door for the possibility of "standing in two worlds."

Reference

Young, J. (ed) (1996) *SAGA: Best New Writings on Mythology*. Ashland, OR: White Cloud Press.

CHAPTER 6

Standing in Two Worlds: Inner and Outer Realities

Introduction

Once trust has been established and underlying feelings associated with the trauma and loss begin to be expressed, a new awareness emerges of "standing in two worlds." It is now possible to safely express the feelings as well as many parts and pieces of the content associated with trauma. Such expression is fraught with ambivalence as the choice to control associated feelings and cognitions becomes less possible. During this point in community settings the unexpected becomes the norm. Children as well as adults may find metaphors and actual experiences form immediate context and relationship to the truth.

"Standing in two worlds" represents that time in the healing process when the inner reality of underlying pain and grief may emerge. Whatever losses have occurred in terms of leaving the culture of origin or experiencing trauma and the abrupt interruption of normal life may now join the present moment in creative as well as verbal expression. The past is easily triggered and at times becomes a conflictual part of the present. Separate realities can now co-exist. Defenses that once guarded against the expression of underlying fears, conflicts and feelings have lessened and the past can now be recalled safely with moments of review, anguish, conflict and new levels of acceptance and possible integration. The outer community becomes the safe container in which to express these realities and to feel less alone.

This chapter explores the reality of how individuals stand in two worlds regarding their underlying grief and loss. Often people experience a relief as the energy consumed in repressing and withholding is released. Again utilizing the Multicultural program, America's Camp and Creating

New Identities in the Work Place will serve to illustrate the power of this process.

Multicultural Program

A Korean girl tells a folk tale from her native land: "The Snake and the Man." Once a man was taking a walk when he saw a snake that was eating a bird. The man shot the snake and the bird was free. Later on the journey it was getting dark and the man was hungry and tired.

He found a house. He went into the house and asked the woman if he could get some food and stay the night. She gave him some food and said that he could sleep in the barn. Later that night the woman came and had transformed into a huge snake. The snake said the man had killed her husband who was a snake. She tried to kill the man but stated that if the bell rang four times he would be saved. Suddenly a bird rang the bell once. It caused the bird to lose its beak and the beak dropped off bleeding. The other bird that was the partner rang the bell three more times and his life was spared. They rang the bell to save their children from the snake and the snake became a woman again.

Children begin to share tales from their own country of origin and combined tales from their homeland and the dominant culture. One such tale combined a reference to Cambodia with a western fairy tale. Cambodian children shared the tale of how they made their way to their grandmother's house during the monsoons. Combining their own stories of surviving monsoons with the fairy tale of "Little Red Riding Hood," they traverse two cultures. Only with the help of a sea turtle who carried them on its back were they able to navigate the flooding waters making their way to their grandmother's house. Reaching the other side their grandmother's house was built on tall stilts and was able to withstand the storm. Once inside their grandmother offered them food and sustenance.

After attending the Cambodian New Year celebration at the Center for Cultural Exchange a facilitator created a poster with pictures highlighting aspects of Cambodia. One of the girls pointed to Ankhor Wat and the other temples and shrines remarking that she liked them. She then pointed to the pictures showing people working in the rice paddies, rubber plantations, fishing on rivers, and selling goods in the market places. "I don't like those, they are embarrassing. The kids at school would tease us."

Several Sudanese girls were doing body tracings. As they created clothing design and added facial features and other details they chose a blue-eyed, blonde-haired American girl.

After they traced each other's bodies children were asked to create design and color for body features. Many of the group members actually turned their body tracings into western culture features. Discussion that followed found many of the children, including the artist of the drawing shown in Figure 6.1, adamant about the fact that this is indeed a picture of herself. Such personal inclusion of western style, fashion, hair color and design shows the need to adapt to the dominant culture.

Figure 6.1: Body tracing

My Grandma,
She died when I was two. I didn't even saw her. She died in Kenya. My mother told me one time her hair was so long and smooth. Down to her waist. She died when there was a war. My mother had to run away. They ran in all different directions. And even my grandpa. He ran. That was in Kenya. He got away. And then he died. Later in the war. I think their spirits are in heaven. My mom said her father used to like her very much. My mother does not have pictures. They were lost in the war. My brothers and sisters were born in Kenya but

Figure 6.2: My grandma

me, I was born in my country. Sudan. But then my dad died. I was seven. The people came and they killed my dad. My mother and us, we had to go to Egypt. I stayed there and went to school until I was nine and then I came to Portland, Maine. And then I went to Ms. Avedson's class. My dad is tall in my memory. He told jokes like "knock-knock" jokes but in a different language. Arabic.

Once upon a time there was an old woman who swallowed a fly. Then she swallowed the spider and then she swallowed a bird, dog, cat. She came into my dreams and swallowed your head and swallowed a horse, a pig, and then a cow. She pulled my hair. She is a witch. And then she made a magic broom and swallowed a whole bunch of people. She swallowed the sun and the world. She swallowed the stars, universe, angels and she even swallowed herself. And then she died.

Figure 6.3: The woman who swallowed a fly

Monkeys, tigers, lions, dogs and cats. My rat died. He was very old. We bought a cat. We gave the cat to our Grandmother. We can't take care of cats because my mother hates cats. We had a fish. Very old. In January, it died. Me and my brother buried it in the woods. My dad bought a dog in February or October, and we had to give the dog away because it was very mean to people. When I went to see my dog, it barked at me. It didn't know me. I was sad. My goldfish died. And my brother Viebol got a bird. His friend didn't want it. My mom said, "yes we can keep it". My brother was so happy.

Figure 6.4: Animals that died a long time ago

The tales, stories and images shown in Figures 6.2, 6.3 and 6.4 are symbolic of the constant influence between the past and the present. Children in the Multicultural Program well illustrate the constant weaving that occurs in the acculturation process of staying connected to their own culture while integrating aspects of the new culture. Interestingly enough this weaving process is very similar to what happens when children relate the past events of trauma to present life situations. Successful integration at both levels relies on creating spaces whereby the access to underlying knowledge is allowed to be present.

America's Camp

Traci Malloy, resident artist at America's Camp, facilitates art-based community events each year at the camp. These art events involve every camper along with cabin counselors and other interested staff. In Year Two the Center for Grieving Children and Traci had both conceptualized a project of creating a quilt. The third year of camp centered on creating a sky scape. This painted mural sponsored involvement from campers to memorialize the person they had lost. "Apollo's Ascent" was the fourth-year art project. This project supported the children in creating mono-prints and block prints. Children wrote letters to the people they had lost on the back of one of their prints. All prints and letters were attached to three weather balloons and released in a camp-wide ritual. In Year Five the community art-based project focused on a sculpted phoenix whose feathers were created from children's drawings that illustrated people that they held in high esteem or honor. In addition to the sculpted phoenix a giant egg was constructed. In a community ritual the phoenix was elevated. Lights were turned off and its drawn feathers glowed in the dark. Below, the giant egg glowed as well. Twenty-eight Counselors in Training (CITs) had created 300 origami cranes. Ranging from age 15 through 17, these CITs had returned to America's Camp wanting to give something back to younger campers. Reciting a poem and oral presentation, the CITs reviewed their experiences with younger campers and shared the paper cranes. Each of the cranes had been inscribed with a positive message of support to every camper. Books will hold the original drawings while the phoenix will become another community art exhibit.

Each of the community art-based projects collect children's perceptions of both their camping experiences and of the unavoidable truth concerning their personal losses. Unprecedented, such community-based art experiences capture both the present camp experience and the past highly complex trauma. The following images (Figures 6.5 and 6.6) are examples from community-based art that portray the notion of "standing in two worlds."

Figure 6.5: America's Camp quilt

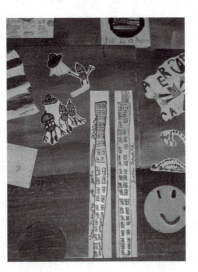

Figure 6.6: Sky scape

Creating New Identities in the Work Place

"Standing in two worlds" group members began to review internalized perceptions of the outer world. Both negative and positive perceptions of the outer world interface with low self-esteem, trauma history and the struggle to reflect on any positive alternative. Mindful exercises focus the group on ways of appreciating the simple pleasures in their present life. Such rituals as morning coffee, walks into nature, viewing the sunset, time spent with children and life events associated with basic living begin to uncover and reflect on the inner values, beliefs and reasons for feeling positive. During this time in the group process short stories from literature are shared as a catalyst for individual and group discussion. Providing both the creative and reflective space to engage in such positive energy often creates the emergence of forgotten yet significant inner resilience and strength. Guided imagery further accentuates re-discovering the inner resources for change.

During guided imagery group members were invited to take one last look at their life stories. Next the guided imagery took each participant on an imaginary walk into the forest. First participants were asked to find a place where they felt a sense of safety and comfort. Once they were comfortable each person continued on their walk, meeting a wise person. The wise person was described as someone who was kind, compassionate and had their best interest at heart. Based on their life stories, this wise person would help them understand at a deeper level what true intention or strength underlies their ability to survive and change. Constant attention throughout the guided imagery was focused on what each participant could see, hear, smell, feel, touch, experience or imagine.

Grace, who had previously shared her fearful story of crossing a bridge, exclaims that the wise person in her guided imagery turns out to be her mother. As her mother comes closer on the path, Grace imagines being surrounded by beautiful flowers and white doves. Her mother reminds her that many of Grace's positive attributes and strengths would not be possible without going through the trials and tribulations of her difficult life. The bucolic scene coupled with the emotional support of her mother helped Grace to feel a positive connection to a more hidden truth. She could begin to imagine standing in the present world with unconditional support and love.

Another female group participant had previously shared her poetic expressions. Writing both poetry and children's stories, she revealed an empathic highly sensitive ability. Sharing with her peers, she illustrates story after story of how this same sensitivity has become her Achilles heel. In social settings she has frequently extended her empathic sensitivity toward people who have either taken advantage of her or been abusive and demeaning. She has developed little self-awareness of the dangers and liabilities of such gifts. In her guided imagery she imagines finding a huge pile of leaves for protection and support. As she imagines a wise person, she is greeted by divine light. The wise person is a male who points to nature identifying in non-verbal ways that she should share her sensitivity with people who would appreciate it.

David, who has previously described his difficulties with authority figures, talks a great deal about how safe he feels with his present partner and family. David finds the outer world at times conflictual and therefore avoids taking risks. He has many personal and professional skills and abilities with little capacity to assess his own strengths. During his guided imagery David finds himself on a large rock. According to his description this rock is a safe and comfortable place where he is able to look out over the rest of his world. A wise person greets David by joining him on the rock for personal counsel. This person helps David to understand that he does feel safe and stable and at the same time is somehow stuck. As they spend more time on the rock the wise person helps David to understand that he needs to calm his own mind in order to tolerate some change and transition. Further counsel uncovers the fact that finding a job matching some of his skills and abilities will help him to feel greater stability with himself and his family.

Conclusion

The transition between the inner and outer realities is fraught with constant challenge. Finding the ability to stand between two worlds means confronting prevailing fears and ambivalence. Re-discovering the inner and outer resources for such navigation requires reflection and the ability to re-focus. Establishing safety and trust for such exploration is critical to the outcome. Within community-based groups an atmosphere of open support and empathy enables individuals and peers to persevere. What is essential at this stage of healing is the ability to trust moving in and out of opposite realities. Such movement supports and corroborates potential consolidation. The interplay with various aspects of the self and of self-perceptions of the world results in formulating new vistas and understandings. Awarenesses increases as such new formulations become more visible.

Mythologically, the importance of the existence of other realities moves the attention from a singular focus to a more expansive focus. Standing in two worlds gives hope that other elements are at work here and that assistance as well as interference have some greater connection to a picture that we can never totally see. Getting assistance along the path may come from entities, people, animals etc. that we may not easily anticipate. If we are open to other realities then the possibility of greater good, a more expansive truth, may be possible.

Tired and hungry, Hansel and Gretel feel hopeless until a white bird directs them to a cottage in the woods constructed of sweet delights. At first the children believe that they are in heaven. The witch who first appears on crutches provides them with comfortable beds and all the food that they can eat. What at first appears to be good fortune soon turns into potential trauma and tragedy. Understanding that they are dealing with good and evil, the children soon gain the inner strength to combat the evil intentions of the witch.

As other realities come into existence, the possibility of referencing the past into the present and imagining a future, becomes achievable. Ineffable realities and feelings are now able to emerge.

CHAPTER 7

Realities Become More Visible

Introduction

It is self-evident that the resources, needs and insights necessary to navigate through significant losses are always found within. Once the necessary trust and support have been established, children go to their inner world of life experiences, and have the ability to imagine and ultimately reconstruct new outcomes, insights and resolutions that were otherwise unavailable. Playing with such realities is not necessarily instinctive. In fact, play is a learned construct. This factor makes it critically important that healing environments offer peer as well as adult models who willingly embrace the highly evolved sensory intelligences of childhood.

Children have been our greatest teachers. The child's wisdom and ability to play with the joyful and painful aspects of their life has been a central thrust in their ability to heal. Grieving is a natural response to change, loss and death and each person has the ability to discover their unique path through their grief process. Honoring and expressing feelings without judgment assists in the grief process and in creating community.

The focus of this chapter is to underscore what happens when community-based programs support the expression of grief within a culture that is both empathic and open to the creative exploration of the often dichotomous realities between the inner and outer world. Freedom both to explore such realities and to create new insights and awarenesses constitutes the foundation of making new perceptions visible.

Re-visiting each group, the reader can expect to gain insight as to how a deeper resolution occurs as community-based participants become less anxious and fearful about owning and expressing what previously was withheld. This evolution will be observed through the Multicultural Program, America's Camp and Creating New Identities in the Work Place.

Multicultural Program

Talks about the Killing Fields in Cambodia, the wars in the Sudan, the civil wars in Somalia, and the tension and conflict in Iran all emerge in moments that blur the space between peers within the community and the facilitators. This opens the challenge to be present with these events and the feelings that come with them. Ultimately joining the pain and conflict that these events stir in the hearts and minds of the children, in their families and in ourselves becomes essential.

The conflicts that arise between children and their separate realities as well as facilitators and their expectations are unavoidable. Such conflict often requires deeper inquiry and exploration in order to join children and offer them the opportunity to change. Underneath such turmoil often lies the hidden past and hidden feelings related to loss, grief and acculturation.

Action-centered, both the non-verbal activities and the symbolic images are open for a child to communicate to him or herself and others about vague, non-verbal, essentially ineffable feeling experiences. With the building of trust, the exploration of feelings and the confrontation of behaviors, children become more visible. At this point entry into the more conflictual past, present or imagined future becomes possible. Such opportunities can appear instantly as a result of the increased safety and trust. Expecting the unexpected becomes the norm. Going with such opportunities is a challenge to facilitators. Integration is beginning to occur, when the present can be quickly referenced to the past or future.

Children's individual stories

A 16-year-old Somalian boy creates two images from clay. One is a key chain holder with abstract images and a personal ring (figure 7.1 and 7.2). Next he creates, utilizing a coil method, a goblet-shaped cup. Within the group, discussion is centered around childhood hiding places and memories of their homes in Somalia and Ethiopia. Together the adolescents talked about the people they have lost in wars and how they miss their families of origin. Bad news, such as the death of friends and family, is usually communicated through letters. People who have died fighting in civil wars are honored.

Figure 7.1: Key chain

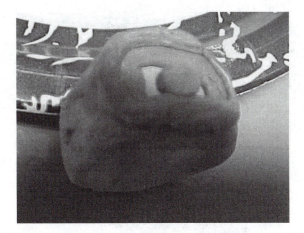

Figure 7.2: Ring

Upholding the respect and memory often translates into not talking about the nature of their death. While the boy worked with his hands on the cup, talk continued about speaking English but still thinking in Somali and dreaming in Somali as well. As he smoothed the rim of the cup he reflected on his father's death. As the oldest son he would be expected to do some of his father's practices within the family. At this point he joins his mother by helping with household tasks and helping with younger siblings. He talked about the things of the future that his father would never see, like his marriage etc. All the while his slender hands continued to fashion the cup as he told the story of his mother breaking a cup that she could not replace. He wanted to replace this object in an effort to help his mother. Now he talks about the losses related to his father who will never be replaced.

Another adolescent from Somalia talked about relatives who have died in wars in his homeland. He has two cousins who were killed in such conflicts. Holding an illustration board on his lap he draws an image that is out of view for the rest of the group (figure 7.3). Later he shares with the other males that this is a drawing of his father who died when he was five years old. He is not clear about what took his father's life but still has some early memories of his father. He recalls that his dad disappeared for several days; no one knew his whereabouts. Four days later a friend brings his father home. His family learns that his dad was in an auto accident. His father died two days later because there were no medications available for his injuries.

Figure 7.3: Portrait of father

A 17-year-old Somalian adolescent has multiple colors of sculpting clay in his hands. With a great deal of ease he is carefully sculpting a multicolored animal (figure 7.4). His hands work quickly and he has a remarkable skill to craft the smaller details of this animal figure. Soon it becomes clear that the animal is a bull with horns. He shows his bull to the group and talks about

Figure 7.4: The bull

himself and his family running for their lives through the streets of their village. He shows us a scar on his arm from a bullet that grazed him during the run. He also talks about a man in front of him who had his arms badly wounded and about running over people who have been killed. He says that the fact that you have feelings is just that. No one is left unaffected as collectively we enter moments of this civil war in Somalia. Connections are made with trauma that cannot be easily integrated and yet the bull looms, majestic like a symbol of this adolescent's strength and faith in his ability to survive.

In a mixed boys and girls group of children from Cambodia, ages 9–12, the children created clay sculptures. Several of the children created clay pots using coil and pinch methods and remarked on how their pots could be used to plant seeds. Following their lead the facilitators secured flowering plants and during the next group meeting the children put plants into their clay pots. Talk emerged about the parallel between nurturing and caring for the plants and nurturing and caring for themselves. Collectively children talked about what it feels like to be uprooted or transplanted. A lot of sharing took place as children looked at the pots that each other had made. A planting was made for two members of the group who were missing. Within the group there were exquisite moments of peace and silence as the children worked co-operatively.

An adult Cambodian language and educational assistant accompanied the children to the Center's program. She has many insights about the children and is highly skilled and perceptive about some of the Cambodian children's experiences. She shares about how many of the children's parents escaped and survived certain conflicts and massacres. However, many of their family members did not. As a result many of the children react to the parents' stories as well as to their silence. Many Cambodian parents choose not to discuss the past, or their feelings with their children. Consequently their children live with the fears and the apprehensions of unresolved trauma.

Becoming more visible, children are momentarily in touch with the traumatic or nostalgic past and at the same time more present with the process at hand. The more their own culture is freely accessed and supported, and the safer they feel with the invitations into the dominant culture, the better understood and accepted they feel. To that purpose children were invited into the Portland Museum of Art. At that time "Sebastião Salgado: Migrations", a photographic exhibition of humanity in transition, was being shown. The children from the Multicultural Program were invited into the museum's studio in order to produce art that described themselves and their family in transition.

A ten-year-old girl from Vietnam reminisces about not being able to graduate from her high school in Vietnam. One is struck by the honor and pride of her longing. She exclaims that she has always dreamed of being the person in her picture. In detail she describes how the hat, the uniform, and the beautiful red scarf are personally important and socially recognized. The orange hat is symbolic of her religion. The hat and dress are made by hand (figure 7.5). The dress is called "aodia" and is considered both beautiful and symbolically important. The "tag" on her chest identifies her school, classroom and her name. The red scarf stands for a leader who is good, smart and knows all kinds of things. She imagines wearing the beautiful white dress floating in the air while being recognized as an outstanding student.

Another Vietnamese girl draws her image of an American family on vacation (figure 7.6). She imagines that the family is on the beach. Accordingly, they are American people who all look happy, have no school, and have no work.

After much struggle a girl of the Muslim faith draws an image of a heart (figure 7.7). She declares that it is impossible to represent her family members as human figure drawings, however she represents her love for all of them in the form of a heart.

Figure 7.5: Self portrait

Figure 7.6: Family on vacation

Figure 7.7: Heart

A Chinese girl draws an enlarged landscape from her country of China (figure 7.8).

Figure 7.8: Landscape of China

A Sudanese girl draws an image of a grave site. She conceptualizes the spirit of her relative in the form of an angel (figure 7.9).

Figure 7.9: Spirit of relative

A girl from Thailand draws a beautiful landscape with flowers (figure 7.10). She recalls a memory of riding on the train sitting with her mom and still remembers how beautiful the landscape was. This same girl later shares in her group that when she came to the United States with her father and aunt, her mother was still in Thailand and was soon to follow. Unbeknown to the girl, her mother died shortly after her departure. She was told one year later, as children in Thailand are told about death when their elders feel that they are ready.

Figure 7.10: Landscape of Thailand

One child from Somalia recalls how chaotic her transition was from Africa to the United States. As she formed images, she covered them with color and finally created a muddy brown mixture. This image seemed to match her emotions and thoughts at that time (figure 7.11).

Figure 7.11: Image of transition

A Cambodian girl recalls a temple, a village, a forest and a place where you can get water. Although she was born in California she knows a great deal about the beauty and detail of this sacred place. Her mother has shared countless personal stories and details concerning her life in Cambodia. (See Figure 7.12; picture located in the upper right-hand corner at the end of the exhibition.)

A teenage Somalian girl talks about her grandfather being shot to death while she was being held in his arms. In her dreams she still hears gunfire and experiences the feelings of danger. She still worries that her grandfather may never have been buried. A male adolescent talks about his family being threatened by the wars in Somalia, and fleeing through the streets at night. He feels safe being here but wishes that he could still have his native country and his native food with him. A ten-year-old Somalian boy talks about children being taken into the war. He still has dreams of being stolen from his family. Another Somalian boy talks about catching his mother's purse and hiding it, because it would be stolen by war members who act like police. Even though he feels safe in the United States, he still worries and dreams about the military coming in to hurt his family.

Figure 7.12: Cambodian temple

Together the children talk about the need to have peace in the world, to stop the fighting, guns, and all the bad, terrible things that happen to people. Somehow, many of the children at times imagine that they have control over all of these horrible things and that through their minds they can stop it.

A beautiful image of a mango tree spurs talk about how in Vietnam sour green mango is dipped in sugar. Children started creating flags of their native homelands of China, Vietnam, Somalia, Sudan and Iraq. Some children discuss Ramadan and other cultural and religious holidays and talk about how they practice certain holiday rituals. At one point music became a topic of discussion. As a result music from various cultures was brought in to share and dance to. One boy's group decided to utilize rap music as a backdrop to creative movement and dance as well as verbal rap about coming to the United States. A boy from the Sudan talks about the wild rabbits in Africa and how the hyena is the most prominent animal. Further talk reveals that there are certain men who are able to tame and capture wild animals in nature.

One girl talks about how she and her family had to leave her brother behind in Somalia. Her brother is still there and lives with her aunt and uncle. She still thinks about him every day and wishes that he were here with her. Her father tried to stop the fighting and was killed. Her brother is her best friend and she dreams about him. She plans to do a memorial for her father who died when she was born.

Children from Somalia talk about their extended families of fathers, mothers, aunts, uncles, sisters and brothers who live in the same home within an extended family. They talk about how wonderful life was in a family where people shared responsibilities. Some family members cooked, others did childcare, while others went out to work. The stress started when family members were killed when going outside of their home. No one even knew who killed as the killings were done silently without warning.

America's Camp

In its fifth year of operating, America's Camp has fully embraced a dualistic philosophy. The Center for Grieving Children's facilitators, "buddies," have truly become consultants to the bunk counselors. Although America's Camp is not a grief camp it has fully embraced the reality that children have highly individualized and complex issues regarding the loss of their parents and relatives in the line of duty from 11 September 2001 and other disasters. Father Peter Rancourt opens and closes camp with a clear message that all campers have experienced death and grief. Second, America's Camp gives full attention to providing a rich and fun camping experience for all children.

All counselors and helping staff have begun to embrace the concept of expecting the unexpected. Both in training and consultation the anticipation of encounters with campers' grief and complicated feelings have dominated discussion and role playing. The outgrowth has been more normalization of grief and other related topics. Within the cabins, amongst peers and within the broader camp environment children are more spontaneous in discussing their losses and in sharing significant things about their lives.

Shared camp concerns

Younger campers who at this point were aged seven and eight had been two and three years of age when 11 September 2001 occurred. Their memories are based on the family myths and stories that have been shared with them. Many of these children have older siblings at camp. It is common to hear older campers share stories about helping their younger siblings to understand what their missing parent was like and what some of the complicated issues were surrounding their death. At the same time these same children are playing out the tragedy through art, play and creative expressions in the art project and at Buddy Central. Because they have no actual memory of it they struggle with trying to comprehend such complicated grief.

Older campers who are now 17 and 18 are returning as Counselors in Training (CITs). This group constitutes 32 campers who have made the conscious decision to return to camp as assistants to counselors and other staff. The significance of their involvement symbolizes the positive nature of their connection to America's Camp. Many of the CITs talk about how much they want to support and connect to younger campers. During the camp's closing ritual the CITs shared a poem and talked about what America's Camp has meant to them. At that same closing ritual all of the CITs created paper cranes and wrote positive messages inside them. All 255 campers received their personal well wishes.

Camp rituals such as staff training, opening camp fire, community-based art, Father Peter's waterside gatherings, MTV night, closing banquet, and closing rituals have all embraced both the celebration of children and camp life and the acknowledgment of loss and grief. Integration is reflected by the leadership as well as individuals who share specific stories, music, poetry, art, dance and drama.

Creating New Identities in the Work Place

Within the group process individuals become more aware of themselves and their inner resources and therefore more cognizant of the integration between the positive aspects of themselves and their work possibilities. Inventories, such as the Meyers-Briggs, further underscore learning and communication styles. (The Meyers-Briggs is a personality inventory based on the work of Jung and of Meyers and Briggs. This self-assessment offers an understanding of natural preferences and reveals whether a person is an introvert or an extrovert, an intuitive perceiver or a sensing perceiver, a thinking decision maker or a feeling decision maker, and people who show their thinking or feeling judgment in dealing with the outside world versus people who show their sensing or intuitive perceptions in dealing with the outside world.) Grace was able to identify her strengths and skills in her ability to be a Certified Nurses Assistant. Her good communication skills and her empathic capacity made such work meaningful and successful. Grace truly embraced her mother as her guardian angel. Never again would she feel alone or without solace in facing difficulties and conflict. Within the group

Grace was able to accept people's support and to offer her own insights to others.

Anne, who is in her thirties and has two disabled children, re-discovered a lot about her own inner strength and ability. She was able to present some of her difficulties with her son and his therapeutic and educational needs to the Children's Cabinet. Through this process Anne received specific and helpful recommendations. Her dedication and devotion to her children was remarkable. She followed through with each recommendation and was able to secure the help that she and her children needed. Anne had a deep and passionate love of nature which included her garden, a goat, chickens, a dog and other animals. She delighted in celebrating this gift with her children and friends. Because of her children's needs Anne was able to secure childcare and a job with evening work hours. Through her self-exploration and group work Anne easily identified her aspirations to be a Certified Nurse's Assistant or an advocate for children in special education. Her increased self-esteem and her positive attitude about her new job at a local discount store were notable.

Jim who is in his mid-thirties had a partner with two young children and a baby who was born prematurely with complicated health problems. Jim easily identified himself as a devoted father. He enjoyed playing with his children and was deeply concerned about his new infant daughter. In his life story Jim was able to identify his grandmother as a person who gave him a great deal of love and support. He well recalls her words of encouragement. Jim experienced a great amount of anxiety. He was able to identify a strong interest in cooking. In fact he recalled learning cooking from his grandmother. In her later years he actually did much of the cooking for her. Jim was able to re-connect to these positive early recollections and was able to transfer his interest and abilities with cooking into culinary employment.

Conclusion

Becoming more visible, children as well as adults were able to more effectively integrate the past, as well as their future, into their present experience. Having built safety and trust there is more willingness to take risks and to forge into the unknown. The inner world as expressed through imagery, stories and affective language is more readily available. In the fairy tale "The Queen of Tung Ting Lake" the lead character Chen finds himself initially trying to find his way home. The magical quality and beauty of both the women and the island that he finds himself on allows other realities to emerge. Soon Chen discovers the truth about his compassionate rescue of the seal and the fish. What at first seems like an unfamiliar reality soon uncovers Chen's true destiny. He becomes more visible to himself and therefore accepts the privilege of the new relationship with the queen's daughter and the elegant surroundings of which he feels more deserving.

There is a willingness to take risks by recognizing inner truths in both activities and social connections. By being more present opportunities emerge whereby more spontaneous action and thoughts can be expressed. This enables the individual to become more visible and therefore leads to letting go.

CHAPTER 8

Letting Go

Introduction

Observing the transformation of grief, it is impossible not to recognize the number of ways that individuals transform perceptual realities by letting go. Often it becomes necessary to re-play certain aspects of the grief process until such a time occurs when either the content can shift or the process itself can end. Discovering that individual perceptions are flawed or somehow connected to false guilt and misunderstandings opens the door for forgiveness and letting go. Recognizing that one is not alone provides additional support. Liberation is further accelerated by being able to healthily release anger and anxiety associated with grief. Often the initial content of trauma and resulting fears and anxieties need to be symbolically and experientially released over and over again until they can be let go of.

Embedded at a deeper level in the structure of this book is the belief that human vulnerability is both the seat of human trauma and the throne of human empowerment. The ability to seek empowerment or to rise from the ashes of disenchantment, shame and human suffering give us the opportunity to step back from our fate and to realize that there is power in creating outcomes and recovery. Standing back from the traumatic events that both shape and predict life circumstances allows the individual to develop new strategies to release and express the truth thereby gaining the human power to let go and transform.

With little support to engage in such realities or to feel free to let go, the child's way seems yet another course of vulnerability. The child's sense of pleasure over principle still allows for the belief that change and transformation is possible. Sensory-focused, the child's play which isn't necessarily natural but needs to be reinforced does not represent a path of wisdom and knowing as much as it represents a natural path whereby the unconscious instincts and realities can be encountered and played with. Directed by the body of experience, such action-centered responses provide release for the emotions as well as the psyche. Dream-like, such experiences also resonate with the neurological need to transfer such information from the memory stored in the amygdala into the prefrontal cortex where action-centered activities provide new insights and connections with previously learned material and memories.

The child's strength is to be present with the affect and emotional content and to go to the body and heart for the lessons which can get played out through play, art, drama, dance, sound, puppetry, story and the like. To dare to take risks by telling the truth on a journey into the unknown; and to be free of expectations, attachments, or predictions of the outcome. Such ingenuity needs to be supported, encouraged and made safe within the context of a safe place and trusting relationships.

Shamanic traditions, the medicine woman and medicine man in indigenous and eastern societies and cultures, have taught how to trust the inner path. The patterns of these traditions maintain a connection to the mythic structures that support creative expression, health and adaptation to change. Providing a model whereby a community of individuals can feel the support from leadership and from their peers both to witness and to share the truth of their life stories is a healing place where collective myths and truths can freely emerge. Paying attention to what has heart and meaning and accessing the human resource of love becomes paramount to such a process.

Across all cultures there are four universal healing salves: singing, dancing, story telling, and silence. The stories, songs, dances, rituals and prayers of humanity re-awaken and sustain the divine child both within our communities and within ourselves. Paying attention to individual life stories re-awakens the sense of awe, hope and possibility. It is how such stories are illuminated and heard that honors the resource of human love and universal support for change and transformation to occur. The dreams and visions that can be shared in trusting communities have the capacity to take humanity closer to the core values, ethics, wisdom, and insights in order to create collective meaning.

The Multicultural Program, America's Camp, and Creating New Identities in the Work Place are exemplary of such trust and safety. Each program is strength-based with particular attention to mindful body-centered rituals and activities. Each participant is highly respected and honored. Implicit in such understanding is the acceptance of each participant's ability to discover healing in themselves and thereby the ability to let go.

The Multicultural Program

The Multicultural Program at the Center for Grieving Children well portrays the structures that are necessary to promote integration and change. The more opportunity within this program for children to participate in cultural experiences from their own countries of origin or from the dominate US culture, the more opportunity there has been to name and personally describe their feelings relegated to the past, present and their imagined future. From the rich masks workshop offered by Oscar Mokeme, Director of the African Museum, Portland, Maine, to the opportunity to create an exhibition of drawings drawn in the studios of the Portland Museum of Art, portraying children's experiences in leaving their homeland and coming to the United States, participants in the Center's Multicultural Program were deeply supported to express the complexity of their losses and difficult acculturation. Community collaboration heightens the opportunity for advances in both the healing and acculturation processes.

An adolescent girl from Thailand spends several group sessions creating file folders for papers. With each file folder she decorated the surfaces using a stencil brush and multiple colored paints. Soon she became a leader as other group members wanted to join her highly creative process. After several group meetings, suddenly, during the silent activity of decorating file folders she offered to the group a very difficult story. She had left Thailand with her father and other family members. Her mother had stayed behind to take care of details before coming to the United States. After more than a year had passed she questioned her father and other relatives about her mother's whereabouts. Without her knowledge her mother had actually died shortly after their departure. Grief-stricken by the information, she shared her feelings with tears as she told her story. Traditionally children in Thailand are not told about death until family elders feel that they are capable and prepared to handle the truth. Other members of the group were greatly affected by the story and spontaneously shared stories about loved ones that had been left behind.

A young boy from the Sudan draws repetitively scenes from war (figures 8.1, 8.2, 8.3, 8.4 and 8.5). During group sessions he isolates himself and appears to exhibit a low self-esteem. Over time his drawings of war and

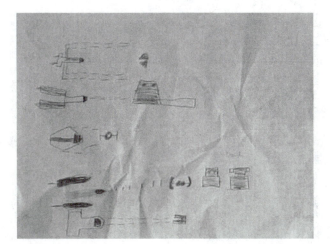

Figure 8.1: War image 1

Figure 8.2: War image 2

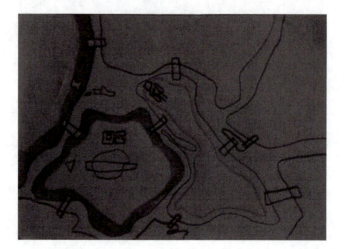

Figure 8.3: War image 3

Figure 8.4: War image 4

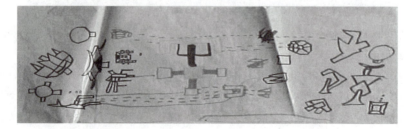

Figure 8.5: War image 5

destruction change to an actual memorial to his aunt and uncle who died two years previously (figure 8.6). Later he creates a sculpted image of a factory which embodies his positive feelings about the Center for Grieving Children (figure 8.7). The repetitive expression of war and conflict helps him to let go and express underlying grief. Within the group process he actually moves from a position of isolation to becoming more of a participant.

This is for my Aunt and Uncle who died two years ago. My Uncle was hit by a car when he was walking and the other one wanted to go to war but he died going from California to Washington.

Figure 8.6 Memorial

This is my factory, where everything is free, it's also a hotel, it's everything. Anyone can come here and get anything for free. It's called the Center for Grieving Children.

Figure 8.7 Factory

Many of the children in the Multicultural Program have had direct experiences with civil wars, refugee encampments, fleeing for safety, witnessing torture, witnessing death and experiencing displacement. For other children such experiences have been encountered through their parents and the stories shared within their families. Any expression of direct and indirect trauma from individuals within the peer group becomes a catalyst for peers releasing their own parallel stories.

In a group of boys from Somalia several children became interested in creating cars. Various materials were used including wood and clay. As each boy became more familiar with the technology of creating a car, they became more creative in creating variations such as trucks, vans and jeeps. While playing with a three-dimensional clay version of a jeep, one boy spontaneously asked how he could create a gun and a soldier on top of his jeep. Discussion broke out within the group about the civil war in Somalia. Boys began to describe how unsafe it was to be in the streets or even outside of your own home. Talk emerged about the difficulty in understanding who was the enemy and who you could or could not trust. Even police and public safety officials whom one would consider trustworthy became the adversary. As a result trusting police and other helping professionals in the dominant culture becomes questionable. Such underlying conflict further contributes to acculturation difficulties.

America's Camp

Letting go is a phenomenon that infiltrates the entire camp experience. America's Camp activates the natural languages of childhood. Dancing in the dining hall, singing in the bunks and at MTV night, playing games, doing individual and group art, playing any number of sports and water activities, going to six flags, Jiminy Peak and other amusement parks, playing "Panic," "Mission Impossible" and enjoying free play all provide the opportunity for expression and letting go. Peers and counselors support each other and support campers to take risks, to be creative, to be themselves and learn from their own experiences. Because action is central to most activities, children are natural in using their bodies, senses and minds in a hands-on approach. The positive spirit that such activity builds at an individual and community level becomes palpable.

Children talk more out loud, says Traci Molloy, the resident artist at America's Camp. Traci describes how children worked on their images for a sky mural, sometimes changing them three or four times. One boy constructed the towers with the exact number of floors. Other children drew their dad's tattoo, a red, white and blue star with Engine 21 on it or their dad's firefighter badge. Talk broke out about the body parts that have been found and identified. One girl said that her father didn't die on 11 September but instead he died trying to save others. Transforming their grief children begin to change more traumatic memories and experiences from the initial trauma into more heartfelt memories and perceptions of their parents before the tragedy. Such transformation and identification with more positive earlier recollections is a primary example of letting go.

As mentioned in Chapter 6, during Year Four at America's Camp the community art-based project was focused on creating foam board prints on colored paper. This project was facilitated by Traci Molloy and entitled "Apollo's Ascent." (figure 8.8) Completing art prints, the children selected one in honor of the parent that they had lost. On the reverse side of the print personal messages were written. Three weather balloons were secured and all the prints and messages were attached to the guide ropes. A ritual was created with Father Peter Rancourt saying a prayer and two counselors from New Zealand doing the Huka (a Maori dance used in New Zealand for weddings, funerals and celebrations). Another camp counselor read a poem. On previous afternoons the weather had been cloudy with periodic rain. On the afternoon of the ritual the clouds separated over the field where 220 children and over 300 staff members gathered for the event. More than 350 images rose into the afternoon sky (figure 8.9). Five hundred and twenty people were silent in honor of the moment. As the balloons became airborne the afternoon sun glinted on their surfaces. Dream-like the community collectively felt the spiritual significance of this letting go. Spontaneously, once the balloons were out of sight the children wanted the rope cut in order that they could fasten it around their wrists.

Creating New Identities in the Work Place

Within the group process, letting go is related to the point at which participants are individually or collectively able to release old myths about themselves. The group process focuses on the deeper truth of each person's strength and ability to persevere through the trials and tribulations that have negatively shaped and impacted their lives. Many of these perceptions have been inherited from one generation to another. Often such perceptions have

Figure 8.8: Art prints

Figure 8.9: Apollo's ascent

been greatly influenced by trauma and abuse. Difficulty in managing self-care and decision making are highly symbolic of low self-esteem. Within each group process are mindful exercises focused on recovering the positive elements in daily life. Helping participants to regain a positive sense of even simple acts such as a morning cup of coffee, a walk into nature, reflection on poetry, pleasure of eating, relaxing sounds and metaphors and finding safe and trusting relationships begins to shift negative self-talk and thinking into the positive realm. Creating decision-making trees helps individuals to begin to organize their approach to such daily problems as childcare, transportation, financial needs and prioritizing the decisions that can be made when alternatives are available. More positive energy gets developed individually as well as between group members. Openings occur whereby negative standards and measures can be released, reflected upon and re-focused.

Tammy, who went public with her story, talks about the struggle between her need to believe in herself and the possibility of work juxtaposed to the family welfare myths that she grew up with. According to Tammy she grew up with the belief that welfare was something she should hold on to, not something that she should try to leave behind. Furthermore, family members and friends reinforced that if she was no longer eligible for welfare then she would not ever regain the benefits that she presently held. At age 37, a single mother of three, Tammy had been on welfare for her entire life. Having successfully worked for over a year, Tammy now reflected that many of her friends and family were afraid to leave a world that wasn't very satisfying but had become predictable. Letting go of these earlier myths and perceptions Tammy was clearly able to recognize that what fears others held in themselves were located in her. Joined with these insights and her deeper exploration of the abilities within herself Tammy was able to let go of previous myths about the work place. Tammy imagined finding demanding supervisors and an unsupportive work environment. The work opportunities group process, facilitated by a rehabilitation counselor, Work Opportunities director and a psychologist who co-ordinated with a career resource specialist, supported Tammy in discovering strength-based realities about herself and supported her job development and placement. Much to Tammy's surprise she actually found her work supervisor to be supportive and helpful. Tammy also generated a positive relationship with her work partners. Tammy was able to experience her success in the work place and was very aware of her own ability to let go of old family myths and perceptions.

Jim, who is a man in his mid-thirties, shares with the group the details of a problematic pregnancy that he and his partner are presently experiencing. Their prematurely born infant requires constant medical care and attention. Jim shares a great deal of worry and concern not only regarding his immediate situation but also regarding his life in general. Jim reflects that he is grateful for what his parents and grandparents have taught him. Growing up, he spent a great deal of his life with his grandmother. Jim actually took care of his grandmother during her later years. According to Jim his grandmother would tell him "You can do it so stop saying you can't."

Within the group Jim shares the many negative and worrisome feelings about why he is unable to work. His negative self-talk had become routine in the group. Only occasionally would Jim reflect on some of his positive attributes. In actuality he was a devoted father, sincerely concerned about his new infant daughter, empathic about his partner's needs, an excellent cook, technically skilled in computers and very loving and positive about his children. Jim was able to find employment as a cook at a local restaurant. Yet, within the group he continued to complain about every negative aspect of the work place and his supervisors and obsessively reviewed the mistakes of those working around him. Members of the group were able to supportively remind Jim of his grandmother's positive encouragement. At the same time they confronted his negative thinking patterns. Brainstorming collective recommendations were made concerning how Jim could observe better boundaries while giving himself more positive support within the work environment. Jim was able to start letting go of the more habitual patterns of self-doubt in light of the group's support.

In the same support group, Anne, who is her early thirties, experiences learning deficits and insecurities in the work place. Conflict resolution was nearly impossible as Anne felt inadequate and often without the skills of her peers. Anne has two elementary-school-aged children both with special needs. She has made every effort to secure therapeutic and educational support for her children. With all of her efforts Anne was feeling very blocked in the pupil evaluation process (PET).

Anne recalls from her own childhood that she was without support and encouragement in her educational endeavors. She believes that she was able to prove everyone wrong. Anne remembers not receiving support from most of her teachers. After high school graduation Anne went on to trade school and successfully graduated in early childhood education.

Anne presented her problems with the PET process to the Children's Cabinet who generated very specific plans, strategies and professional contacts. Anne followed through with the recommended plan and successfully made gains regarding her sons' special educational needs.

Anne became successfully employed on the night shift of a large wholesale store. She chose the night shift in order that her children would receive ongoing parental care and support. She also arranged for her children's grandmother to provide overnight childcare. With resource support on the job, Anne was able to maintain her work schedule and to work out any conflicts with management.

Anne uncovered an aspiration to become a child advocate. She wanted more than anything to promote local Olympics that would be offered for disabled children. She was well aware that such a career would require additional education and work experiences. Anne felt very strongly that her present job was exactly what she needed to provide the support for her family. Her long-term goal would be to pursue her deeper aspirations at a time when her children had completed their formal education. Anne was highly regarded in the group for her good decision-making abilities and for her mature attitude in considering her family's needs first. Anne seemed easily able to let go of her primary aspirations with a belief that she could fulfill this need at a later time.

Conclusion

Spontaneity is at last possible as the ability to be more present emerges. Individuals in all of the groups begin to take action on changing perceptions of themselves by actively letting go, thereby enabling them to gain new insights, awarenesses and connections to the past and to the imagined future. Defenses are now less operational and there are more opportunities for taking risks. The freedom to openly share insights and acknowledge the past allows for a new level of integration.

As a result of his father's death Sindbad inherits great wealth and many estates and possessions. However, due to his lavish life style he wasted his wealth and rich inheritance. It wasn't long before he became a pauper. He then decides to become a sailor on a merchant ship. As the story goes Sindbad the sailor encounters one adventure after another. He eventually recovers his great wealth because of his ability to let go of one reality, enter another, and find his way to ultimate freedom.

Through insights and expression come resulting change and the ability to let go of previous patterns and behaviors. In community settings the ability to share feelings from the heart, to perform collective acts of kindness, to experience collective rituals and activities of celebration and sorrow results in letting go and enables integration. The realm of possibility emerges as human empowerment leads to enlightenment and hope.

CHAPTER 9

Hope

Introduction

The child perceives the world both in the context of the culture which adult models and relationships have presented to them and through the innate intelligence that they bring to life itself. Inarticulate about putting words to more imaginative and unconscious awarenesses, the child soon learns to conform in some ways to the outer standards of the family and culture. The ability to trust deeper perceptions and awarenesses that are relegated to the world of dreams, play, imagination and make-believe, are personal insights into the unconscious and more uncensored authenticity. Such personal insights gained individually or within groups results in the acquisition of new insight, new abilities, new love and new appreciation for hope and change.

In Antoine de Saint-Exupéry's book, *The Little Prince*, he illustrates this point well when he describes his six-year-old perceptions of reviewing a fabulous picture book entitled: *True Stories from Nature*, a book about a primeval forest. The book revealed the truth about a boa constrictor swallowing its prey whole, without chewing, and sleeping for as long as six months in order to digest it. Thinking deeply about the adventures of the jungle, Exupéry writes about the effort that he took to draw such an event. Showing his drawing to adults, he asked if they were frightened by such realities? In dismay, most adults confused by the image immediately remarked, "Frighten, why should any one be frightened by a hat?" (Saint-Exupéry 1971, p.4).

His drawing was not of a hat but instead he had tried to illustrate a boa constrictor digesting an elephant. Going further with his efforts to communicate such realities to adults, Exupéry portrays a drawing from the inside of the boa constrictor so that adults could see the elephant. The grown-up response was to admonish his efforts and to advise that he set his drawing activities aside and pay more attention to the academic learning of geography, history, arithmetic and grammar in order that he might better understand the real world (see Saint-Exupéry, 1971, p.4).

Disheartened by his efforts and the failure of adults to understand Drawing Number One from the outside of the boa constrictor and Drawing Number Two from the inside of the boa constrictor, he resolves that it is tiresome for children to continue to try to explain things to adults who never seem to comprehend such matters. As a result he chooses not to pursue drawing and painting and instead becomes an airline pilot. Utilizing geography he can easily distinguish China from Arizona.

An adult himself he has lived amongst grown-ups but this hasn't improved his opinion of them. Whenever he met someone who had any in-depth appreciations of the world he would show them Drawing Number One. When they recognized it as a hat, he would never discuss important topics like boa constrictors, primeval forests, or stars. Instead he would talk about politics, bridge, golf, or neckties. Such discussions would appeal to their sensibility.

Many years late, flying alone, his airplane crashed in the Sahara desert; survival became critical. Awakening the next morning our narrator meets the little prince, who comprehends Drawing Number One and Drawing Number Two and demands that the survivor draw a picture of a sheep. Admitting that he has had to concentrate on his studies of geography, history, arithmetic and grammar, he admits that he no longer knows how to draw. Not taking no for an answer, the little prince insists that he use his imagination and produce a picture of a sheep. Exhausted by his many fruitless attempts, he draws the sheep in a box. The little prince exclaims that that is exactly the way he wanted it drawn and so the story begins. The little prince who is a being of enlightenment meets our narrator who is crippled by his conscious identity.

Truly the passion and strength of who the narrator is has much more to do with the divine child. His awe and wonder about boa constrictors, primeval forests, stars and other planets have much more to do with the underlying meaning of his life than his outward abilities to fly, to know geography or the like. Unable to meet another adult who can relate to such mysteries, he meets the little prince who enjoys and ponders on a much deeper, more enlightened level about life.

Very few adults either understand or appreciate Drawing Number One or Drawing Number Two. The familial, educational, political, cultural and social boundaries and structures of the adult world have created a mythos that prohibits such acceptance. Underneath, remaining unexamined and often unexplored, is a mythos that forms a relationship between mankind and nature in a more connective reality. A reality that is interwoven with awe and wonder as well as sensuous meaning and context. The reality of Drawing Number One and Drawing Number Two offers the individual connection to a world that engages the person both to understand and discover the outer and inner realities of why we are here and what we need in order to feel the support, love and connection to our hope and higher purpose.

Gifted with new insight, new meaning and new abilities, hope emerges in the form of change. Following are examples from the Multicultural Program at the Center for Grieving Children, America's Camp and Creating New Identities in the Work Place that illustrate context and reality of changes of self-perception.

The Multicultural Program

A group of young Cambodian girls and their facilitators attended the Cambodian New Year celebration at the Center for Cultural Exchange. Later the group explored highlights about aspects of Cambodia. The children talked about the importance of the Cambodian temple. Ankhor Wat was a very important temple and the center for a great number of family celebrations and rituals. As a result of the discussions several of the girls performed Cambodian dances which required complex hand and body movements. During the dance performance children would look at the dancers intently as a form of spontaneous support and trust. Throughout the year children had made requests for American foods and cooking. However, at the end of the group process the children spontaneously requested Cambodian foods. Cambodian fried rice and other Cambodian ingredients were bought at a local Cambodian store. The children led the facilitators in both the shopping and the food preparation. Openly the children taught the facilitators Khmer words and more about the native foods that were cooked at home. The freedom to integrate more cultural language, foods and activities signaled the open ability to integrate more fully the past with the present. At the same time conversation about food preparation and dance movements was a catalyst to the discussion of how these traditions would be included in their future families.

Simone, who is a Cambodian translator and advocate for children, became an important catalyst for change and hope regarding many group members. Personally she exhibited a very kind and gentle spirit towards the children. Often Simone would participate spontaneously as an additional support to the group process. A young Cambodian boy who had experienced a lot of moves and transitions along with the loss of several siblings struggles in the group process. In a picture story drawing he draws a story about himself finding an egg. He picks the egg up and discovers that it is a turtle's egg. Making a castle for his imagined turtle, he creates a special home for its comfort and care. In his imaginary land the turtle sleeps on his bed, eats fish and swims with him. Simone interjects that children don't often get the opportunity to play and express themselves anywhere else.

Continuing to express himself through imaginative play this same child creates elaborate animal masks. These masks include a tiger, a lion and a wolf. The animals take on monster-like qualities. Playing with the masks, themes of helplessness and overwhelming fear get played out in relationship to the animal masks. Such regressive play brings out more and more of this boy's sense of helplessness and his need for support and reassurance.

Within the same group Simone shares that her father and two brothers were killed in a war in Cambodia. Listening intently this same Cambodian boy shares that his mother frequently talks about a lake that is full of dead people and that there are such negative spirits there that no one goes near.

During several sessions he releases a lot of anxiety through the use of clay. Ultimately he constructs a Cambodian house on stilts. He talks with great enthusiasm about how the house is constructed that way to be protected from storms and harsh weather. Having gained a lot of additional support from Simone and other group facilitators he is now better able to be more self-assured and a contributing group member.

At the end of the group process he shares a card designed for the adult facilitators thanking them and everybody at the Center by stating that he will never forget everybody. Ultimately he has gained hope by redefining his own inner sense of safety and well-being. Simone brings a cultural diversity to the facilitation that greatly increases the opportunity for the children to gain breadth of connection to the past, to their culture and to not being alone in the struggle for integration.

An adult focus group facilitated by Grace Valenzuela, Director of the Portland English as a Second Language Program (ESL), and the Center for Grieving Children brought together the multicultural community in order to look at the rituals and practices observed regarding death, grieving, mourning and how these practices relate to men, women and children in their own culture.

The result of the meeting and subsequent working groups was the construction of a report regarding such rituals and practices as they relate to the following countries: Mexico, Peru, Sudan, Somalia, Cambodia, Japan, Croatia, Yugoslavia, Russia and Vietnam.

The outgrowth of community collaborations with adults and children regarding specific rituals and practices surrounding birth, death, healing, spirituality, creativity, social, political and educational foundations is the groundswell for hope and possibility. The more frequently that cultures of origin have the opportunity to interact with the dominant culture the more outgrowth there is regarding successful integration, new insight, new meaning, new knowledge and new abilities to navigate together.

America's Camp

Creating a symbol of hope the Phoenix Rising became America's Camp's fifth-year community-based art project. With over 255 children and the largest staff ever, the entire camp, along with the direction of Traci Molloy, created a phoenix bird with a fourteen-foot wing-span. Traci, with the help of many hands, created the wire and papier mâché bird. The children, counselors and other staff members created water-based pastel and water-based colored pencil images. The images portrayed the honoring of people who had been important and positive mentors in the children's lives. Most children honored their deceased mother or father. The original images have been compiled into a gallery book while color photocopies of the images were cut into feathers and attached to the mythical bird. All of the children's images were attached to the underneath of the phoenix, while all of the counselors and staff images were attached to the top side of the bird's wing and neck.

In addition to the creation of the bird, a large egg was also constructed. This egg was filled with over 300 paper cranes that were constructed by the Counselors in Training (CITs). These adolescents who were previously campers at America's Camp now have a heartfelt need to give something back to the younger campers. Many of the campers are their own siblings or siblings of their peers and friends. Each CIT not only created paper cranes but also wrote a positive, encouraging and hopeful message on the inside of the folded paper cranes.

At closing ceremony the mythic phoenix was placed in the field house at America's Camp. When the children arrived all of the house lights were out with only stage lights illuminating the bird. Unknown to the children the bird had not only been covered with their personal drawings but had also been covered with a special translucent glow paint. As the entire camp of children, counselors and staff surrounded the bird, Traci Malloy stood at the center of the circle and addressed the camp. Heartfelt, her message was eloquent with the direct way that she spoke to the children. She reflected on the project and how the children throughout the years have continued to honor and memorialize their dead parents and relatives. What was even more elucidating was her conceptualization of the power and magnitude of children's ability to share their deepest feelings and thoughts with themselves and with each other. She spoke about the resilience that she observed in the children's ability to openly express their feelings about loss as well as their feelings of love and hope for the ones that they have lost. Empowering children further, Traci observed that when camp starts each year the adult counselors, staff and volunteers give openly their love and support to the campers. In many respects the adults feel a need to protect and provide safety for the children. In essence it is her observation that the children actually enlighten the adults as they bravely express themselves verbally, artistically and socially around the issues of their lives and their transforming grief.

As the phoenix was elevated above the children, the bird glowed in the darkness as it freely turned, casting an almost mythical appearance in the closing ceremony (figure 9.1). When the house lights were turned on the large egg was removed from the dark material symbolizing the ashes. The CITs gave a talk about what America's Camp had meant to them and recovered the cranes from within the egg, giving each child a paper crane with a written message of support.

Creating New Identities in the Work Place

As has been seen in Chapter 8, Tammy Herrick was able to let go of many of the family myths that she grew up with concerning welfare. In this chapter more of Tammy's story illustrates her ability not only to let go but also to

Figure 9.1: Phoenix rising

find hope and deeper resources for change and transformation. Tammy recognized that the fear that was so evident in her family members was also evident in herself. In his book *American Dream* (2004) Jason DeParle follows several welfare families. He observes that most of the people in his study have skills that would serve them well in the working world, but they are held back by self-doubt and by systems and agencies that continue to focus on deficits and problematic behaviors rather than strengths and internal resources.

Tammy, a 38-year-old woman who has never been in a work situation, shares how her mother never talked about work as a possibility. In fact, after living in foster care for years, she and her sister returned to live with their mother. Tammy said that her mother always lived off the state and currently lives on Social Security Disability. Her mom told her, as Tammy left the house after giving birth to her first child, "How are you going to make it, if you don't live on the State?" Although she felt loved by her mother there was never a model presented by either parent about the emotional, financial or community benefits of work. Tammy disclosed to the group that at one point she was suicidal, and if she had not joined a church, and specifically a church choir, she would have succumbed to her depression.

Within the group process Tammy was able to address problems with her adolescent daughter by presenting her situation to the Children's Cabinet. The Children's Cabinet are a group of professionals within the human services agency who provide collaborative assistance to group members through direct consultation. Tammy followed through with the recommendations presented to her from the Children's Cabinet. Furthermore Tammy was able to develop problem-solving skills and readily made new decisions regarding self-efficacy. Once employed with "On the Border," a Mexican restaurant, Tammy established new rituals with her adolescent daughter. She encouraged her daughter to share in household responsibilities, established a weekly allowance and met her daughter at the end of her work day for a cup of coffee and review of the day. She was delighted about how her own changes in attitude were affecting her daughter. Furthermore she taught her daughter and son about how to prepare certain Mexican foods at home.

Internally through her autobiography Tammy was able to identify personal strengths and abilities. Her original drawing and verbalization of her life story and the ways in which she survived uncovered personal resilience along with a passion for singing. Tammy was convinced that as she gained financial security through work, she would give more of her time toward leading a girls' choir at her church.

Each of these changes certainly increased her self-esteem and even more remarkably decreased her sense of fear and apprehension about the work place and the outside world.

One woman recalls that even though her family was in constant conflict and chaos, her mother somehow knew how to create order. At the end of each day, she would say to her children, "It's about time that we go to the park." It was during such times that this person recalled her mother's support and love and the beautiful natural setting of the park itself. At times she would beg her mother to not go home, knowing that the time at the park was the safest most connected time between herself, her mother and her family.

Reminding ourselves that it is often the small things that matter, other group members recall significant turning points. One group member talks about how she walks to the river and how restorative such times have been for her to feel the healing effects of the natural beauty and the movement of water. Another woman recalls being locked in closets as a young girl, being removed from her biological parents and being placed in foster care. She eventually is cared for by her maternal grandparents who protect her and give her the support that she needs. Many people recall not being safe and not feeling loved. Yet, throughout the life stories there are moments, even sustained times, when they did feel safe, protected and important in the world.

As people identify their source of connection and their ability to have hope, they also identify their strength and resilience. It is this same strength that often becomes their "Achilles Heel." One group member talks about her sensitivity. Her poetry and concern about her son, nature and empathy for others reflect this sensitivity. Unless she takes care of this ability and shares it with people who appreciate these skills then her feelings can be triggered and she can be scapegoated by others who can put her down. A male group member knows that stability and security are top on his list, but he is unable to take risks and will not leave his home. He cannot discover new possibilities for employment and generativity unless he takes the risk to move outside of his comfort zone in order to explore opportunities.

The three Rs (Rest, Reflect, Re-focus) become a concept that can be used at times when people's feelings are triggered or they are overwhelmed. Most group members have had significant traumas in their life. Their ability to move out of a reactive response is paramount to their ability to pursue a job, to maintain friendships, and to sustain their focus. Rest, Reflect, and Re-focus becomes a standard, well-understood phrase within the group.

For most participants reacting out of anger, needing to control life situations and being unable to take in criticism or rejection makes life unpredictable and work impossible. As each person's stories get enriched and are made more and more visible, so also are their strengths and vulnerabilities. Interestingly enough, vulnerabilities and strengths go hand in hand. The more each person feels comfortable managing their vulnerabilities, the better able they are to move forward in identifying their passions, interests, strengths, talents and true intentions. Self-efficacy is critical in the search for meaning. The program makes links between individuals' stories, their natural abilities, inventories that assess interests and strengths, networking both within the group and with specific needs concerning childcare, transportation and the like, and working with Vocational Resource Specialists to explore work opportunities.

By teaching people that their own life story holds the meaning of their lives and holds the potential for future possibility and resilience, we open the door to change and transformation. The issue of Post Traumatic Stress

Disorder is common for people who have utilized welfare. Affect regulation is also difficult for this population. The tendency to respond in an alarm state and to project anxiety in every moment is common. People in such states do not feel entitled. Quite the opposite, they suffer from a form of human oppression that leaves no door open to imagination, nor to possibility. If people are able to overcome these barriers, they must feel trust and the safety to explore and expand their understanding of themselves.

It is how such stories get illuminated and heard that honors the resource of human love and universal support for change and transformation. Throughout this 12-week program participants not only get to tell their life stories and be heard, but more importantly get to re-discover the roots of their own resiliency. Interestingly enough most of these memories emerge from childhood. Developing the skills to self-sooth and to safely hold their own feeling realities becomes critical to the change process. Networking within the group, helping clients to create networks within the community, creating decision-making trees and teaching some rudimentary goals with mindfulness reinforce patterns of self-efficacy. Ultimately the challenge is not to avoid feelings being triggered as much as it is necessary to have strategies that help you to not repeat the same patterns. Both at work and at home there is an opportunity to change myths that were previously unexplored and to navigate in a world that holds both hope and opportunity.

Conclusion

Throughout each community-based program it is evident that hope is closely accompanied by the inner ability to change personal myths. At the same time the transformation of trauma and grief is possible as a result of the difficult road to enlightenment. Letting go of personal attachments to the traumatic events themselves, to the need for control over them, to stop creating personal blame and shame are prerequisites in discovering hope and possibility. Being open now allows for new insights, new meaning, new knowledge, new abilities and new love.

Connections are now possible. Insight occurs more naturally as there exists the possibility of integrating previous experiences with what is occurring now and the ability to look positively and optimistically to the future.

In the Chinese fairy tale "The Queen of Tung Ting Lake", Chen, who was an ambitious young man of great intelligence, succumbs to the enchanted realm of an island where women rule. The queen of Tung Ting Lake and her beautiful daughter help Chen to leave behind his identity of poverty and servitude. At the end of the tale Chen encounters his boyhood friend Liang. Chen declares that since he hasn't been home for ten years Liang is unaware of the changes in Chen's life. After this meeting Liang returns to Chen's native village and discovers that according to his friends Chen is dead. Left with unanswered questions multiple realities emerge. New connections between the old and new myth of who Chen has become leaves the reader in a heightened truth. Interfused with both the beauty and awe of Chen's new life signals a letting go of previous perceptions and beliefs. From a penniless student he has become wealthy beyond measure and married to a beautiful and elegant lady. Throughout his own quest for life and meaning he has progressed not by wealth but by good deeds. Ultimately he has become more wealthy and gifted by being truly who he is. Letting go of previous realities, Chen has been able to discover hope and transformation.

References

DeParle, J. (2004) *American Dream: Three Women, Ten Kids, and a Nation's Drive to End Welfare*. New York: Viking.

Saint-Exupéry, A. (1971) *The Little Prince*. New York: Harcourt, Brace and World.

CHAPTER 10

The Authors' Autobiographical Exploration of the Importance of Myth in Creating Personal Reality

Introduction

Throughout the book, we have emphasized the importance of childhood. In this chapter both authors talk about their own childhood and growing up experiences. For one of the authors, home was the South-East of England, for the other author, rural Maine. We talk about our early childhood memories, and the importance of our families and local communities.

Even though we were born in very different parts of the world there are a number of similarities in our experiences. For example our home lives were very loving, supportive, nurturing and caring. This provided us both with a firm foundation in which we could then go on to tackle whatever confronted us. For so many of the individuals we write about in this book, that foundation was not present. Both of us experienced personally and professionally loss and trauma. These memories, stories and images have remained with us and have enabled us to go to these painful places with the children and adults with whom we have come into contact. The early establishment of safety and trust in our own families of origin allowed for a great deal of freedom, exploration, play and fun. Experimentation with imaginative as well as tangible realities allowed us the ability to take risks. We both experienced the diversity of cultural differences. Through our travels and the people that we came into contact with, we developed a greater understanding and respect for

individual differences. These could be in the form of different family traditions and values, foods, languages or even religious practices. These were not
issues to be fearful of, rather they were opportunities to learn from.

Regarding our professional careers, again each one of us was encouraged, supported and nurtured. Doors were opened. Yes, we had to go
through them and make the most of the opportunity, but we benefited from a
great deal of support and understanding. What is significant to both of us is
that somehow we never forgot the people nor did we ever lose sight of where
we came from. Our childhood and formative years had a deep and profound
impact, which has stayed with us until this day and continues to guide our
professional careers.

One of the authors immigrated to the United States in his mid-twenties.
The other author grew up in an immigrant family. The popular "misconcep-
tion" is that the United States is a very tolerant place. Yet, in reality this is far
from the truth. Both authors experienced the complexity of integrating two
cultures, two languages and the different ideologies that such backgrounds
present. Within our families the myths that we were taught had specific
tenets linked to our parents' cultural heritage. Our ability to traverse such
unique realities while living in a dominant culture presents internalized conflicts that are not easily voiced. We frequently felt as if we were standing in
two worlds. Both of us came from "working class" backgrounds. Our grandparents had worked in professions that were defined by physical labor. There
was a myth that one had a position or station in life. People were not
expected to leave their home setting or environment. Although both of us
have left our homes of origin, what has not left us is where we came from and
the importance of those working-class values and traditions. At a certain
level collective realities such as taking care of your family, standing up for
your brother or sister, the importance of good deeds, respecting your elders,
working hard, doing your best were the imperatives taught by both the
culture and the family.

In addition we have both been in settings where the learned personal
myths were not helpful in seeking healing or wellness. Thus the ability to find
hope and ultimately change requires a letting go. The roots of transformation
are always linked to personal and collective truth. Honoring self-expression
and uncovering what lies beneath the silence is relegated to non-verbal languages. We both feel that the direct access to play, nature, art, imagination,
stories and the like not only filled our childhoods with meaning and purpose
but also is the foundation for human empowerment. We were both taught that

anything you do for others, your community, your family, your friends does count. In essence good deeds create a better world. These values and myths reflected on the deeper interconnection between the self and others as well as the self and an ever expansive natural world. Like the fairy tales of Peter Rabbit, Hansel and Gretel, Cinderella and even the rhymes and riddles of Mother Goose our childhoods were filled with the acknowledgment of other conjoint realities. Interdependence was a concept well practiced within our family life, our immediate communities and the cultures that we were attached to.

Finally, the reason why both authors feel it is important to tell their own stories is because most adults have discarded the roots of their own lives. They view them as childish, immature and relegated to the past. We totally reject that philosophy; rather we believe that childhood experiences are of paramount importance and continue to be a part of the present moment. Being able to learn from the past while being fully engaged in the present allows for future hope and change.

Immigrating to America: Paul Johnson's story

Early childhood

For the first 26 years of my life, home was the seaside town of Southend-on-Sea, its claim to fame being that it had the longest pier in the world, and that its mud flats had apparent great healing qualities. It is located about 30 miles south-east of London on the Thames estuary. I was born on 24 November 1959 at Rochford hospital. On my birth certificate it said Father's Occupation: railway clerk, Mothers Occupation: housewife. As a child my mother repeatedly informed me that when I was born I was not expected to survive. Apparently, there was such concern about my survival that I was baptized on 25 November, and my parents were told to expect the worst. Well would you just know it, I confounded them all, and am pleased to report that 46 years later, I am still alive and kicking.

Regarding my childhood memories and experiences, I was the eldest of three siblings, having a younger sister and brother. I can still recall the first home in which we lived until I was four years of age, the layout of the bungalow, the large back garden, the weeping willow tree and the swing in the garden. I can also recall going for walks with a gentleman by the name of Mr. Richardson. He would take me down some wooded pathway to a pig farm where I could hear the pigs grunting and squealing.

I can also recall taking my sister's hand and walking to the local stores around the corner. To this day, I tell the story of how my mother would send me at the age of three and my sister aged one to the local stores. Talk about child labor!

Middle childhood

When I was age four we moved into a bigger house, which was located on a new housing development. As a child you couldn't have asked for anything better. There had to be between 30 and 40 houses on this development, and all of them appeared to have children of varying ages. So, school holidays were spent out playing on the street. You would go out after breakfast and play until lunchtime. Go back out again after lunch, go in for tea, come back out again until 7.30pm, and then start the whole process over again the next day.

No one ever seemed to worry about where their children were, or whether they were safe. The only time I think I would need to see my mum was if we decided we were going to the local park, which was some five minutes away. That process involved going into the house and shouting out "We are going to the park." One of the games we used to play was soccer, where we would pretend that we were a particular team or player. We would also play cricket. Another particular favorite was "ten pan alley," a game of hide and seek. Two people would have to count to 100 and then have to find everyone else. Some of the hiding places would be in people's garages, back gardens, or behind and under cars. The games would go on for hours.

Family culture and traditions

There is no doubt that I came from a loving and caring family. While money may have been tight at times, it was made up for in so many other ways. As already noted, I was the eldest of three, my sister being two years younger than me and my brother six years younger than me. I can still to this day recall the day my brother was born, 20 January 1966, and walking into the bathroom, where my father was shaving and him saying to me: "Go and see what we have." There was this beautiful baby boy, fast asleep, his hands held up either side of his head.

I guess that was one of the qualities of my family, we all shared in one another's successes or disappointments. Just because you were an adult or older than someone, that didn't make you more important. I firmly believe that this factor plays a major part in my social work career that has enabled me to see everyone in a similar light. It didn't matter who you were, you had a right to be seen and heard. Where did this perspective come from? Well, I would have to say that my family's church had a major impact upon all of us.

It appeared there wasn't a day when someone in my family was not at the church. This was the epicenter of our social and community life. Again, to use a social work term, this was our eco-map, everything evolved around the church: youth organizations, choir practice, Christmas bazaars, social evenings, church meetings, harvest festivals, etc. Whatever the reason, my family was there.

I would have to say that this egalitarian approach spilled over into our home. Everyone was treated equally, everyone had something to contribute, and no one was seen as being less worthy. I can also recall as a young child Christmas days and my grandfather dressing all three of us and us putting on a performance for the rest of the family. I can also recall every summer from the age of seven onwards going to spend a week at our grandparents' house in Watford. My grandparents lived in a council house at 319 St Albans Road. I can still to this day visualize the layout of the house, what was in the rooms and the different smells in each of them. For example, the kitchen, my grandmother cooking sausages in the morning and the aroma filling the entire house. Also, watching my grandfather shave at the kitchen sink and the smell of his shaving foam. The smell of coal from the coal shed that was located in the kitchen. You could tell if a storm was coming by how strong the coal smelled.

I can also recall how punctual they were. Breakfast was at eight, dinner at one, tea at five. My grandfather slicing and buttering brown bread. Also the way in which he would make a pot of tea, warming the pot first, letting the pot stand and then adding the tea. Each summer my sister, brother and I would spend a week with our grandparents. It seemed like each day had its own routine. Monday was always laundry day. Tuesday and Fridays were market days. Each Wednesday, we would always go to Windsor Castle on a day out. Now believe me this was quite an event because we had to take three or four buses as neither of our grandparents drove. Thursday, well, Thursday was a marvelous day because that was the start of the cricket. I can still recall my grandfather earnestly cleaning and polishing the furniture in time for the 11am cricket match. At that hour we would both sit down and watch the cricket from Lord's or the Oval. Life didn't get better than that!

Young adulthood: coming to America

When I first came to the United States in 1981 I was a young 22-year-old, who was coming to work in the States for the summer. There was something exciting, unbelievable and unreal about the whole experience. Yet, I knew it was just for a summer and after three months I would be returning home. However, what I was not prepared for was just how captivated I was by New York City. It was like no other city I had ever been to. My first experience of New York City was being propositioned by a hooker on 42nd Street. As a 22-year-old and having only been in the country for about an hour, "What a place!" I said to myself. This experience was soon to be replaced by a much more humbling and realistic one.

I was a summer exchange student working at a camp for the mentally and physically challenged in the Catskills. Bus load after bus load of handicapped people arrived. I was assigned two men, both in their mid-twenties, who required total assistance with feeding, dressing and toileting. No big deal, I thought. I would have a good time and the work wouldn't be too strenuous. By the end of the summer I began to see them as individuals not as people who were disabled. I don't remember how many bums I wiped, or how many showers I gave, or how many meals I fed, or how many times I lifted someone out of a wheel chair. All I know is that I had to go back for more.

In 1984, before entering social work school, I worked in a residential program for severely to moderately handicapped adults. Once again I was wiping bums, dressing, feeding, teaching daily living and social skills. If you will pardon the pun, by starting at the bottom, I really gained some first-hand insight into what it must be like to be handicapped.

After graduating from social work school in Great Britain in 1986, I decided to immigrate to the United States. I had approximately $500 to my name and two bags of belongings. Since 1981, I had been coming on a regular basis each summer, working at different summer camps or staying with friends. However, on this occasion there would be no going back. Over the course of several years I had fallen in love with New York City. There was something magical and exhilarating about the place. Yet going to live there, well, that was something very different.

First, I had to get a job! Eventually, I obtained a position with a program for the developmentally delayed, a 52-bed adult Intermediate Care Facility. On my first day at the program several of the staff asked me how long I intended to remain. Why had they asked? Over the past year two social workers had been employed at the program. One lasted two days, the other lasted a week. I soon found out why!

The program had not had a social worker in over a year; so all their bio-psycho-social evaluations were out of compliance. In addition, the program was under state mandates to reduce the size of the population at the facility because it was "inappropriate" for diverse clients to be residing in one facility. For example, the program had mentally handicapped clients, physically handicapped clients, autistic clients, mentally ill clients, and dual diagnosed clients all under one roof.

A year after working at the residence the program went through a re-accreditation process. For the first time in several years the program was taken out of sanction. The auditors reported that the program was attempting to address issues of concern.

The reason I mention this particular story is due to the fact that when I came to the States I didn't care what job I got. I just wanted a job. I had to pay my rent and I needed to eat. In other words, I was living at a very basic level. The other thing I should note was that when I originally came to the United States in 1981, I somehow obtained a social security number. Although I didn't realize it at the time, this was my "meal ticket." With this piece of paper I could live and work here.

Living in America

So here I was, living and working in the Bronx, a setting very different from the town of my childhood and youth. In many ways I was glad my parents and family couldn't see me. I think they would have been somewhat aghast at the living arrangements and the location of my new home. I lived on 296th Street in a three-story brownstone with several others. You had to take the Number 1 train to the last stop and then take a bus. To get to work involved taking three buses across to the other side of the Bronx.

In many respects I was re-living the experiences of millions of illegal immigrants who had come to the United States before me and millions who would follow me. We frequently hear of people escaping their homelands and coming to the States for a better way of life. Well I don't know if "better" is the correct term. What I do know is how difficult the whole process is, and that one is confronted with a whole host of problems that one could never have anticipated or envisioned.

First, there is the feeling of being overwhelmed and getting through the day. It's as if you are powerless. For example, going to the store to get groceries is a very different process. The smells, sounds, the way people walk, talk and think are so very different. And this is coming from someone who had been visiting the country for several years who had only himself to take care of. When getting my first job, the agency involved knew I needed the position. They knew I couldn't make demands over salary, yet somehow they made me sweat it out. Eventually, when I obtained the position as already noted, it was evident that any "regular person" would have turned the job down. But I didn't have that luxury.

The second issue that immediately struck me was how many people treated me as something of a novelty item. "Oh, I just love your accent!" "I went to England once." "Do you know so-and-so in Coventry." "Have you ever met Lady Diana?" "Do you like the Beatles?" On the one hand I was extremely flattered that people would think I would come into contact with such company. Especially as I see myself as a working-class lad who would much rather hang out down the pub with his mates than mix with the high and mighty. But somehow there was something troubling about this.

Another issue that continued to confront me was that when people saw me they would assume that I was a white American male. It wasn't until I started speaking that they realized that I wasn't American. This created a whole host of issues for me. Being British I had a very different perspective on life: I had a different upbringing, I thought differently, and spoke differently. Also, I loved cricket, wanted to know the football scores, and was always on the look-out for an English newspaper that I would read from cover to cover. Also, I was always tuning in my short-wave radio to the BBC's World Service, listening to those magical words "This is London," listening on a Saturday morning at 11.40am to the English soccer results being read: West Ham United 2, Arsenal 2. What bliss!

In my work environment I found it very difficult to be working in an agency that only dealt with one population. In England I had worked in a local authority agency where you dealt with numerous and diverse issues. Also, issues like health care troubled me greatly. I couldn't understand why we didn't have universal health care coverage in this country. I had lived in a country where you were covered from the cradle to the grave. So, for the first three months that I was working at my new job, I did not have any health insurance.

In other words whilst on the outside it must have appeared that I was doing well, inwardly I was in a great deal of pain. As noted earlier, I came over in the summer of 1986, illegally; so there was no leaving the country due to the fact that I might not get back in. Every weekend I would call home and catch up on events and make sure that everyone was well. The truth was that I was missing everyone terribly.

I can still remember vividly my first Christmas in the United States. Thanksgiving had been easy because despite the numerous questions of "Do you celebrate Thanksgiving in England?" there was nothing to compare it to. My response was that America was having a big party in order to celebrate my birthday, on 24 November. Yet, Christmas was very difficult. Not seeing my family, the anticipation during the week before Christmas, not going out to the pub with friends, no mince pies, no Christmas pudding or Christmas cake, no traditional Christmas Eve communion, no Boxing Day, no soccer and no BBC. The list went on and on.

Even today I still miss these events. There is something traditional, cultural, comforting and reassuring about all of them. It's as if it is part of one's being. It isn't until you don't have them any more that you realize how much you miss them.

Conclusion

There is no doubt in my mind that my family and experiences of living in America have impacted on my professional career tremendously. In all the settings that I have worked, intake social work, working with the mentally ill, mentally and physically challenged, child welfare, and victims of physical and sexual abuse, my work has been affected by my personal experiences.

For example, I could never understand why I was drawn to working with the mentally and physically challenged. I just loved working with this population. Other people would cringe at, for example, my work with youngsters in foster care and victims of physical and sexual abuse. I really felt I could empathize with so many of the children and young people with whom I came into contact with regard to issues of loss, feelings of betrayal, powerlessness, and stigmatization. When I immigrated to the States it was as if I became a nobody. I no longer counted, I couldn't vote, couldn't express my opinion. I just had to accept everything. Everything I knew, trusted, believed in and loved was taken away from me. For perhaps the first time in my life I felt really alone. I had no one to call upon. I was abandoned. The bizarre aspect of all of this was that it had been self-inflicted. Yet, with the young-sters I worked with, they used to tell me of their experiences. How they were taken away from their families. How they hadn't seen a family member in several years. That even though they knew they had been neglected or abused, they still wanted to have some form of relationship. That was their family.

In many respects I again could relate to these experiences. I couldn't see my family, I couldn't leave the country. I was powerless. There was this great sense of loss and a huge void in my life. However, trying to explain this to people was not easy. "You wanted to come here," they would assert, "You should be pleased to be here!" The answer to both questions was yes, but it still didn't take away the inner pain and overwhelming sense of loss.

In other words, for most immigrants, the process of migration to a new country is often connected to numerous losses; the loss of one's home and homeland, of community, friends, and loved ones, of familiar food, sounds and smells. Although these feelings are central to the inner core of who I am, they were not easily communicated or shared.

Growing up in an immigrant family: Bruce St Thomas' story

Growing up in a small Maine community I was exposed from Day One to the belief that Natural Order existed. Above all other orders, my parents and extended family taught through their stories and actions a constant, remark-able, respect for nature. Home to me was the Native American towns of Lincoln (Mattamiscontis), Mattawamkeag, Winn, Howland, West Enfield, Passadumkeag and Milo. The folklore and myths of these communities was built on the stories passed down for generations about the rivers, lakes, streams, forests and animals that surrounded these Maine towns. Historical patterns of the interdependency between human life and nature were still observable in this rural geography. Woods camps, hunting and fishing camps, ice houses, fox hunt towers, grist mills, farms, pulp mills, barns, and the like peppered these rural landscapes.

My father was French-Canadian and two generations removed from the province of Normandy in France. My mother was Scottish-English with many generations of family who lived in the land of my birth. Because my own gestation and birth was problematic, all bets were off regarding adult expectations. After a very nurtured pregnancy, which required bed rest and hospitalization, I was born on 23 July 1948 with no significant problems. All was well and my family joyously celebrated my healthy arrival.

My father, a woodsman, and my mother, a book-keeper, were enjoying a happy life in a small Maine town. My brother, who was three years older, was delighted to have a potential play partner. Through the earliest of my memories I can still recall the sounds, smells, images, textures and feelings of that childhood cottage where my father danced on the kitchen floor and my mother read stories, poems, and childhood riddles that to this day are still in my memory. Our cottage was a two-bedroom, one-story building that had an L-shaped porch that formed the living room and dining room.

Patterns of play and time spent languishing in the present moment were superseded only by the timely rituals of my parents departure from and back to our home. Mrs. Littlefield, our housekeeper, pampered me with silver dollar pancakes made every morning directly on the wood-fired cook-stove, and dances that she and I performed through the house to the tunes of the Inkspots, Glen Miller, and Billie Holliday. The music flowed from the wooden mahogany victrola that smelled of records and hot electrical tubes that I imagined glowing on the inside. Oh yes, of course there were the radio programs, like Maggie Muggens, Gene Autry, and the Lone Ranger and Tonto. Outside there were walks through the woods to the pond and walks to the local store. A tall whispering pine tree outside my bedroom window was the spot for afternoon tea parties and quiet play. And there was the wood shed and a huge old barn that provided endless hours of exploration. Life was joyous for those first four years. My father came home from the woods at about 2.30pm, just in time to wake me from my afternoon nap and take me out to the pine tree where he would put me on a branch, sing to me and offer me pine pitch that he had chewed into gum.

My mother returned home about 5.30pm. Mrs. Littlefield had dinner on the stove and my mother would embrace both me and my brother, escort us to the living room couch and read to us something wonderful before dinner. Her perfume and office smells would linger with the story as she read page after page from Grimm's Fairy Tales. I still can recall resting in her arms while her voice expertly played with the words like a concert pianist moving effortlessly and with pleasure across the keyboard.

My own identity somehow was being woven between the simple rituals of my home life, the rich stories and fairy tales, and my direct contact with the people and the abundant natural landscape. Stronger than ever was a notion building that something larger was being transacted that had less to do with logic, and more to do with the natural order of feelings and connections between the heart, human life and a larger world of nature, animate and inanimate realities. I was never alone even in my quiet play. I had a sense that silent entities were by my side and actively a part of my life. Connections were everywhere, and those connections fed my spirit as well as my heart and mind with a joy that was unspeakable.

My father and his family spoke French fluently. My uncle was a French teacher in the local schools. Although we spoke English in our home, my father's broken English/French dialect along with his French ideas and concepts created a bilingual and rich atmosphere in our family life.

My father offered a very different view point. As a woodsman, he created a clear link between the natural and the human world. Because my father was bilingual, I was able to develop very different perceptions of the world. Non-verbally and verbally he was able to present view points that were often in conflict with the culture that I lived in. French family gatherings and celebrations were far more joyous, spirited and filled with rituals of eating and singing and dancing. I adapted to the western culture externally but internally I naturally gravitated toward my father's ways.

A woodsman by nature, my father's instinct carried most life activities into the outdoors where nature provided structure and support for our most playful adventures. I was overwhelmed the first time my father took me into the woods where he and his fellow woodsman were cutting trees with a bucksaw. The combination of massive work horses with nostrils spilling body heat into the frigid air, with men physically manning a woods operation, and with the beauty and smells of the deep forest filled my senses and mind with the awe and majesty of their interdependence.

Articulate in her wide verbal skills, my mother's voice played with fairy tales giving form and shape to the three pigs' houses, delicately holding Cinderella's tragic story and boldly playing with the whimsical character of Sindbad the sailor. As my mother read, my brother and I would be suddenly transported to other realities and to other parts of the world.

Inside I would never know a more comfortable home. The perfect balance between the training of my body and spirit being met with the magical wandering of my mind, created nirvana. The combination was delightful and filled my own heart with the creative ability to find awe in all that I encountered. My father's simple phrases of "what goes around comes around," "give freely and it will return double fold," "no matter what be kind, and imagine being in their shoes," shaped the perceptions that I had of interconnection not separation. Undivided I imagined that every action, thought, and deed was singularly significant and collectively critical. Louis Armstrong's song "What a Wonderful World" boomed from the victrola speaker and I could imagine people singing in the streets "I Love You."

All that I surveyed kept swirling with the love and acceptance of a present moment that although individual, was collective at the same time. Small though my world was, it truly was resplendent with an expansive quality that allowed heaven and earth to co-exist, other realities to be imagined and a playful sense of adventure. No judgment was placed on the quality, the process nor the outcome. It was as if perfect order was the ongoing assessment of all that prevailed. The simple structure of my daily life offered endless opportunity to engage in the beauty, mystery and connection to the life around me.

Professional career

Of significant mention was the three years I spent in the United States Army. I was a low number on the draft during the Vietnam War and found myself immersed in the conflict and psychological trauma of the Vietnam War. I became a mental health assistant and worked closely with quad-amputees, burn patients and psychologically injured Army officers and soldiers. It was my initial introduction to what was called war fatigue (PTSD), trauma and other related sources of inner conflict. What was most significant was how resilient people were especially when they received the loving support of spouses, family, friends and the health support system.

Professional development and training moved me from the Vietnam War to the world of art and psychology and ultimately a doctorate that explored the relationship between art, child development, psychology and counseling theories. Interestingly enough my dissertation was entitled the Action Statement. I explored the importance of children's picture story drawings drawn in action formats. Throughout my career when I ask children to recollect picture stories of the past, present or future, they presented details of their perceptions of themselves and of the world. Action in drawing as well as action in life seems central to the freedom of expressing and learning from life experience.

With over 30 years of work around the issues of childhood trauma, I am still convinced, as I was in those early years of my own youth, that the world is very much interconnected. Children continue to validate this point in their play and through their non-verbal art and creative expression. What is more profound is that children instinctively are knowledgeable about the inner pathways to grieving, to healing, and to human enlightenment. When supported by adult mentors, who build trust and safety, children who are psychically injured, go directly to the voice of imagination to encounter their terror with the use of creativity to conquer their worst fears and feelings, and to reconstruct the meaning and deeper lessons in their tragedy. Trusting this deeper exploration and building a safe relationship with children has become a life-long enterprise. Children understand the silent, deeper truths of human survival. Interwoven in the matrix of nature, creativity, and magic, children form a total and real relationship between themselves, their life lessons and the process of making meaning out of these realities through ritual, play, and the free spontaneous use of materials. Stories that they create are both awesome and archetypal in their ability to transcend conscious structures and to join the more unfettered reality of unconscious order, meaning and insight.

Believing in these processes and in the natural healing power of the child has often confronted me with more conscious efforts that are made in the therapeutic and educational communities and institutions to submerge and discredit these abilities. Non-verbal realities in general are less honored by a culture that prefers words, defined outcomes, competition, excellence, and a need to control learning and development.

Child advocate by nature, my role has brought me quickly into the legal, pedagogical and social fabric of injustices toward children. Standing firmly for what cannot be seen, easily put into words, or consciously resolved has made me feel like an outsider. Although the torch has been carried playing through stories, through community development, through one healing event after another, there is still little support, belief or trust in a process that is so eloquently, instinctively led by children alone and in community. Trusting a child's own ability to discover a course of healing, learning, and developing is still foreign to a large sector of adults in our communities.

Yet over and over the voices of the child leap forward when it is safe, expressing a need to be honored and upheld. In one healing ritual an eight-and-a-half-year-old female child who witnessed the tragic death of her eight-month-old sister creates a magic tunnel out of cushions from office furniture. Within the tunnel she draws a flying tree that radiates electric colors from within its shape and surface. Holding the tree, she exclaims that the magic tree allows her to become anything that she wishes. On the third trip into the tunnel she becomes her dead sister who was tragically killed. Before entering that tunnel she hands me a list of the most unanswerable questions and instructs me to ask the questions once she is safely inside. As I ask the questions, a baby's voice strongly replies.

> "Do you like living in heaven?" I ask.
>
> "Yes," she responds, "There are angels here to protect me and to hold me." Tears form with the intensity of the moment.
>
> "What do you eat?" I inquire.
>
> "We don't need food in heaven," she says with a lightness in her voice.
>
> "Do you still love me?" I ask knowing how critical this question is.
>
> "I will always love you. When you look up in the sky and see a bluebird you will know that I remember you."
>
> "What do you need?"
>
> "I need you to know that I am happy. You should be happy too."
>
> "Why did you leave?"
>
> "Because it was time to go."
>
> "Can I see you again?"
>
> "I will always return to you in your dreams."

No one could create a healing that was more personal or more transformative than what this child created for herself. Bravely, our ability to believe in other realities is our human strength to join the inner resources necessary for expression, reflection and resolution to life experiences that deepen our connections to each other and to a world that we are inextricably attached to. Children exhibit the capacity to believe in the inner voice without questioning its origin or structure.

Conclusion

Growing up in a family where multiple myths are presented from diverse cultural backgrounds sets the stage for a deeper appreciation for the influence that these myths continue to play in personal reality. Opportunity for integration is reliant on the ability to identify with such inner realities and to make such truths known. Being fully in the present embraces both the inner truth of who we are while interacting with the outer connections that give our lives meaning. As a child there existed a freedom to play with diverse and divergent realities. When adults support, participate, and join in such activities there exists a deeper confirmation.

Through my childhood, career and adult experiences I have fully embraced the authenticity of children's stories and creative acts. Therefore I see that children are not passive participants in society, rather, they have active voices and agency in the social world. Because society is primarily organized and ordered by adults and because adults are dismissive of childhood perceptions there is frequently a negative issue of control exercised between adults and children. Very often these same adults have unresolved childhood issues that remain inhibited because in fact they do not have the ability to re-engage through playful childhood resources.

Summary

Autobiographical sketches of the two authors reveal several salient points. Both were brought up in geographically and culturally different parts of the world and yet had some common experiences. They both recall and value the access that they had to play, nature, stories and childhood fun. Interdependence in family life, in the natural world and in myth structures was a common insight that evolved from the safety and trust in their families of origin.

Paul's move to the United States and Bruce's experience in growing up in an immigrant family heightened their awareness of diverse realities and the acknowledgment of an inner life. Their professional development in working with the severely handicapped and traumatized Vietnam soldiers respectively sets the stage for more insight and sensitivity into the conflict between inner experiences and realities and the outer world.

Both authors were aware of other realities than the ones that were communicated through words and dialogue. This larger picture of the non-verbal awareness of integrating into a new culture and experiencing the marked differences between French and American culture opened the door for appreciating separate and often conflicting realities between different cultures. The childhood rituals, games, fairy tales, family celebrations, holiday foods and the like were the many ways in which familiar and cultural myths were both learned and practiced.

Both authors believe that this book deeply identifies and honors the childhood instincts and practices as the natural ground for healing trauma and for letting go of myths that no longer hold truth and meaning when conflict, chaos, and tragedy require the reconstruction of such inner realities. Truly their life stories also represent the strongest belief that adults who can offer unconditional love and support to children actually advance their children's potential for change and transformation.

CHAPTER 11

Conclusion

Empowering Children through Art and Expression: Culturally Sensitive Ways of Healing Trauma and Grief is an exploration of how children alone and in community express non-verbal realities through their own creation. Within this activity is a deeper structure that allows safety to form around the nucleus that we are all a part of a larger picture, a more unconscious mythical reality that connects us to a loving, knowing heart. Without judgment we find ourselves free to be truly who we are without apprehension. It is within this creative process that a deeper reality is revealed. The underlying truth emerges once it is safe enough to go through the complex feelings surrounding life events that were not within our control. Imagination re-awakens the multiple realities within our selves. A new sense of mastery allows us to feel included in the event as well as enlightened by the life lessons that are now available for our inspection.

Using a sensory approach, children utilize non-verbal intelligence to navigate through their life experiences. The translations of their discoveries and insights cannot fall through the filters of the verbal, analytical mind but instead remain mythic truths that stand alone for translation.

Most adults have discarded the roots of their own life myths. Established long ago in the same child-like trial and error crucible these myths evolved from their own personal translations and insights based on their human relationships and cultural heritage.

Avoiding the human vulnerability and pain, many people have chosen to put away childhood memories. It has become too frightening, too painful, too vulnerable to feel again that innocent place of awe, wonder and powerlessness.

Yet again and again children march forward into the primeval forest, alert, prepared, ready to challenge themselves to be open to the numinous, to

share in the joy and sorrow of the promised land. Like a fairy tale, there are
no guarantees, and yet the lore of experiencing the adventure awaits only the
brave souls who move into action. Like the king's youngest son, they are still
open to magic, trusting instinctively that letting go forms the doorway of
opportunity. Guides along the way, real and imagined, form the structure
necessary to discover the truth. Inner connections of both thoughts and
feelings are interwoven with the outer animate and inanimate kingdoms.
Hope remains certain as action creates the constant opportunity to uncover
the deeper meaning and resolution.

Children of different cultures and different life experiences frequently
navigate between inner and outer realities. The conflict of navigating
through trauma along with the differences between cultures, languages and
ethnicities place tremendous pressure on children to acculturate and integrate realities that very often do not easily fit together. However, the
challenge still remains to create a connection that acknowledges the past and
integrates the present differences in a way that supports hope for the future.

Children's hopes, dreams and wishes cross all geographic, ethnic,
cultural and racial boundaries as they embrace the highly vulnerable topics
of human loss, grief and healing. Whether one speaks of children being held
in the Nazi concentration camp of Terezin, or Tibetan children crossing the
dangerous Himalayas to Katmandu to escape the Chinese oppression of
Tibetan culture and Buddhist religion, or children living with the ongoing
oppression or aftermath of war and refugee status from Iran, Afghanistan,
Iraq, Cambodia, China, Korea, Ethiopia, Somalia, Sudan and Vietnam, or
children living with the loss and grief of 11 September 2001, and the loss
and grief of deaths within their own families, there is an observable ability
that children have to embrace human vulnerability.

We observe the deeper sensibility and wisdom that children have in their
ability to move beyond the confines of their own oppression and conflict.
What remains unique is that the children's artwork and creative expression
symbolizes healing and integration. More impressive is the ability to move
beyond the confines of their grief and traumatic entrapment. Unique to each
child's journey and explicit in children's artwork from Terezin, Katmandu,
America's Camp, Afghanistan and the Center for Grieving Children is that
their creative healing was accomplished in community. Establishing peer
communities where children and adults alike believe in allowing and nurturing the natural individual and collective expression of trauma, grief and
healing is a core element in this creative outpouring. Children's imaginative

ability to move beyond the rational confines and understanding of the losses that they have experienced will transport the individual into the multiple realms of where healing takes place.

Gaining a better understanding of childhood resiliency and its role in the treatment of traumatized children as well as traumatized adults is imperative. In his article "Saved from freezing," Norman Fischer, a Zen priest and poet, explores the spirituality of art. According to Fischer, the world and self do appear to us to be frozen. "Our personal problems, our self-definitions, what we hear from those around us—all these convincing and compelling experiences invite us to clutch at concepts, ideals, positions and worries" (2005, p.56). Fischer points out that we build mental and emotional constructs in order to define who we are. Metaphorically he believes that such structures keep the world, and the self, confined and frozen. But the experience of art can shake us free of that; art can save us from freezing.

Fischer believes that spirituality can offer us a larger view of ourselves and the world but can also hit us with an "arctic blast" if we are not careful. In essence, as human beings we crave a sense of self, of security, a truth that we can depend on, a world we can tame and understand. Somehow we want to be comforted by the things that we can believe in even if it becomes problematic. As human beings we do not believe that imagination is more important than knowledge. Quite the contrary, we want our life to be predictable and secure and seek anything that confirms such thinking. Moving away from that reality, art, poetry, stories, play, music and other modes of creative expression take us deeper into the mysteries of life. Such experiences take us beyond the rational world and into larger more significant realities. Imagination takes us quickly into a world that is not dead. In fact, the imaginative world is charged with the elements of rhythm, color, diversity, spontaneity and connection. The imaginative world places us face to face with our highest joy and our deepest angst. It cannot be controlled or forced into mediocrity. Instead, the creative spirit goes beyond the rules, structures and paradigms of the conscious world. Fischer asserts that, "From the viewpoint of the more structured and rationally organized world, imagination is dangerous, for it holds that world in supreme irony, as a mere backdrop for its colorful activity" (2005, p.59). Yet, how as human beings do we make sense of the deeper realities of our life that cannot be put into rational words, or expressed within the context of daily life, or held within our dreams or our bodies as memories and experiences not welcomed in conscious reality?

Survival depends on our ability to make such realities a conscious part of who we are. Creative expression implores that we are a part of a larger picture. Individual power and control needs to be let go of in order that we can better understand our fate and connection to a larger reality that we don't always understand. Trauma and loss frequently triggers such exploration. Commonly held familial and cultural myths may no longer hold the truth that was once familial and complete. Giving up conscious control and preoccupation with the personal nature of tragedy and chaos means letting something else emerge. The truth, always only partial, is revealed slowly like in a fairy tale or in a dream. No one escapes the suffering and pain. Yet somehow being willing to reflect at a deeper level on the moments themselves creates opportunities and choices that were never previously apparent. Art expression, play and creating personal myths keeps the door open for possible change and transformation. Action through rituals and creative expression move the core material at a neuro-biological level as the brain acts as a re-organizing agent in releasing the imprint of trauma. New levels of equilibrium can be established as the brain moves the material from the amygdala to the prefrontal cortex where new insights, meanings and connections can be formed. Previously interrupted action can be replayed and released through the impulse to create some personal freedom by representing the separate parts of the trauma in creative acts, imagery, stories and the like. Ultimately stepping back from the fight or flight response re-focuses the attention toward more open, less contrived notions about the complex world.

Instinctively by nature, we want to form balances in our lives, resolve conflict, be in touch with our desires, know our heart, and bodily release our joy and pain. There are few ways to facilitate the expression of such desires without an incumbent surge of restriction and control. Mythological imagination is portrayed as the goddess, the sage, the genie, the trickster, the muse, the dwarf, and the magician, to name a few. Characters and imaginative entities come forward when needed, sometimes magically to assume helpful roles in understanding the dilemma, to resolve the conflict, to offer direction, and to enlighten the quest. Imagination sustains its energy from a direct confrontation with our deepest hopes, dreams and wishes from our deepest desire, despair and need.

On a more conscious level we often believe that when our dreams come true, or our ship comes in, or the money appears, then and only then will we be happy. Yet, this false hope is a fantasy and even when it does come true, our ultimate challenge is to match this outer reality with an inner source of purpose and need. Fischer believes that we live in a "world of separation and fear, a threatening yet seductive world that promises us the happiness we seek when our fantasies finally become real" (2005, p.59). Imagination confronts desire directly and therefore takes us to the core of its discomfort and intensity, opening the world for a larger view of where we are now. Fantasy and reality are in constant opposition. Imagination and reality are opposing forces. Contrary to popular thought imagination goes directly into reality, allowing for a deeper exploration, shaping, re-presenting, re-experiencing and ultimately uncovering a more profound truth than was previously available. The senses, reason, our intellect and even our moral and emotional faculties are not enough to uncover the underlying complexity and truth of the meaning of our lives. More daring and adventuresome is our ability to let go and uncover the dual realities of what we both struggle with and embrace.

Small children are animistic by nature and have much less trouble visiting and even living in the world of imagination. For them there is no discrimination between the world of matter and the world of dreams. Such realities cross over to one another on a regular basis. Development and the outer world soon teach children to stop such activity and to stay still in order to become a person in some recognizable or organized way.

Childish ways are unpopular. In many respects childish ways have become almost taboo in our own culture because of our need to be overfocused on the material world. Non-material entities are fast disappearing. Even the natural world becomes less appealing as we find fewer reasons to enter non-material realities. The mountains, plants, lakes, streams, rivers, animals and the like are no longer a source of pleasure and intrigue. We no longer have fond names and euphemistic recollections of the stars, sky, the land, the water, or elements of nature made personal by our intimate encounters with them. In the process of growing up we have lost our ability to embrace the ephemeral. Humor, play, magic and imagination are traits necessary for our survival. As Fischer states, "such human abilities help us to avoid the occupational hazard of freezing" (2005, p.59).

Somehow in the warm sun of a March day long after a cold winter, one is encouraged to think of thawing, melting, softening and opening up to the hope and possibility of spring. Working with imagination through art and creativity requires discipline. This is developed directly through an encounter with materials. Children make direct contact with materials, art, play, media, sound, puppets, two and three-dimensional materials and it is through that encounter that inexpressible feelings get formed and expressed and ultimately integrated. Things don't just fall in place, you have to work with the materials, re-shaping yourself to suit them. The dialogue between the materials, the creator and the facilitator becomes the opportunity for catharsis and an in-depth play with the complexity of the rich and highly individualized content of the person's life. We don't need art to know what we think and feel. But without creative expression, what we think and feel becomes static, circular, self-centered and limited. The resiliency of children to go beyond what they think and embrace this human vulnerability is critical and necessary for healing. Because children believe in pleasure over principle, they will often move without thinking into the more active and pleasurable process of creativity. Expression of this nature promotes a deeper awareness and ultimately encourages the development of empathy. Truth as it exists in doctrine and values has to be made more personal. Art provides a way to discover truth, but not the sort of truth that is handed to us already vested. Instead, we must find it ourselves anew. This is a much more difficult proposition.

In many respects the courage to create is the recognition that we are the co-creators of our own myths. We need art in order to promote development and move the inner life. By looking at the world outside of our own personal interests and habits we can feel something of the divine of the whole. In every culture, in every tradition, the human story about who we are, why we are here, what our human needs are and what we are able to give is both compelling and purposeful in the search for meaning. The more that our story is illuminated the more understanding one develops about the true intention and reason to persevere.

When oppression, poverty, and trauma intrude on the course of life, it becomes critical to develop a more in-depth, fuller picture of who we are. Community becomes the safe container, the haven, the vessel of meaning, whereby love and understanding nurture and support the hope and possibility for change.

Throughout this book is an explanation of the child's natural ability, with support and encouragement, to uncover the truth about their woundedness. Utilizing their access to imagination, nature, and animate and inanimate realities, the child discovers a body-centered sensory approach to both express the affect associated with trauma and to create an uncovering, a new integration or perception associated with previous memories, experiences and new insights. That aspect of the child is resilient and flexible in exploring while letting go of outcome and expectation. Such ability is also attached to compassion and creativity. This same gift is observable in adults who can utilize a creative means of re-connecting to the parts of themselves that feel energetic and alive. In fact, it is only adults that present such models to children who promote health and wholeness in community.

The child is an archetype that has been in stories and mythic structures throughout world cultures for at least 2000 years. In her monograph "A pilot demonstration and training project in the therapeutic use of ceramic art with adults molested as children," Frances E. Anderson talks about how incest survivors were in talk therapy for over 15 years with "no resolution of the issues surrounding the incest incidents" (Anderson, 1991 p.3). Dr. Anderson could demonstrate in her study how people in art therapy would begin to deal more directly with the incest issues as well as the complex emotions that surrounded the event. Whitfield talks about healing the child within as being a major thrust in the treatment work. He refers to the child within as "that part of each of us which is ultimately alive, energetic, creative and ful-filled; it is our real self who we truly are" (Whitfield 1987, p.1). "It is when the individual's inner-child is traumatized, stifled and used to meet parental needs that an unhealthy codependent child emerges, that is unable to cope with meeting its own needs or fully functioning as a healthy adult" (Anderson 1991, p.4).

Engaging in art and other creative activities can actually tap into the places where adults have been both injured and resilient as children. Helping people in community to re-connect to the creative capacities is re-engaging the human instinct to uncover pain as well as nurturance and healing. Com-passion, both from the victim and from a community of participants, can re-awaken the ability to uncover new and creative resolution. Human invul-nerability is held as a popular myth both within our culture and within a contemporary framework. The heroes and heroines of Hollywood, the invincible nature of athletes and athletic events, the strength and power of the American image as the superpower come into our lives through TV and the media. At an individual level the myths of perfection, fame, competition, wealth and control over life and death are constantly bombarding our minds and senses. Yet, each and every human being is subject to lessons in vulnera-bility. Little is taught about how to shape, change and ultimately transform the myths that we live by. Somehow our creative capacity to embrace the divine aspects of the child could re-awaken mankind with the ability to believe that change, transformation and healing is natural. The same child who was once injured, abused or traumatized is also resilient in her adult capacity to play with the true meaning of life.

Creating the safety and support for such risks to be taken is the central thrust in the aforementioned stories and programs. Retrieving the inner potential for true self-freedom and flexibility of the inner child is re-awakening the unconditional love and nurturing that was available at certain points in development. If that inner child has been given the love and support to creatively play with life, then that same support can be re-awakened at any point during adulthood. Springboard-like, such energetic and lively material can be re-woven into present reality.

Uncovering the possibility for hope, change, transformation and healing re-awakens the need to re-engage in healthy creative play and the ability to enjoy living. Mindful practices such as the observance of silence, ritual, being present, guided imagery, story telling, singing, dancing, creating art, and the like become the healing salves that act as the vehicle for insight and change. By taking risks and being truthful, each person owns the truth by going on adventures whereby they let go of control and the need to know the outcome.

Each of the stories told in this book represents communities that operate on such principles. Mythic by nature, such community activity is the basis of human change and transformation. A new mythos is necessary if we are able to incorporate the extreme levels of diversity both within our own communities, within the world community, and within the natural world. The tsunami, earthquakes, other natural disasters, terrorism, racism, political upheaval, global warming, fragmentation within political, religious, educational and social structures, and personal trauma presents an unprecedented need to re-discover the underlying collective meaning for humanity. Perhaps the greatest gift for a troubled world is to discover that its most gifted citizenship is represented by the poor, the disabled, the traumatized, the abused, seniors, children, and aspects of the social culture that are capable of creative change and transformation. The health of any nation should be dependent on how well integrated its citizens in need are. To imagine such a goal is to trust that all of mankind truly is equal and therefore contributing in some meaningful way to the good of all.

Such a goal is to trust that our most wounded citizens are faced with a more urgent need to uncover the truth. Stepping into the uncharted waters and uncovering more unconscious realities the traumatized and injured citizens of our communities dare to challenge conscious reality. Universal, such uncovering witnesses the interdependent nature of our human struggle to survive. Like the children of Terezin who imagined positive connections that were beyond the stone walls of their ghetto, perhaps we too need to imagine something beyond the confines of our cultural, political and theological tenets and beliefs.

Throughout this book stories as well as the literature offer one illustration after another whereby community support has afforded children the ability to enter that place where only the creative mind can deal with dissimilar imperatives. Unknown, unfettered, non-verbal, the charge has been to understand and access the deeper unseen connections. For a world that frequently propagates fragmentation and disconnection, we can very much benefit from the child's ability to uncover the interdependent truth. Healing our grief and loss is accomplished by accessing rather than denying human vulnerability.

References

Anderson, F. E. (1991) *Courage! Together We Heal: Mural Messages from Incest Survivors.* New York: MacMillan.

Fischer, N. (2005) 'Saved from freezing.' *Tricycle.* Spring, 56–59.

Whitfield, C.L. (1987) *Healing the Child Within.* Pompano Beach, FL: Health Communications, Inc.

Subject Index

Author Index